I0764257

COMPANION POETS.

ILLUSTRATED.

WHITTIER'S NATIONAL LYRICS.
BRYANT'S VOICES OF NATURE.
HOLMES'S HUMOROUS POEMS.

BOSTON:
FIELDS, OSGOOD, & CO.,
SUCCESSORS TO TICKNOR AND FIELDS.
1869.

NATIONAL LYRICS.

BY

JOHN GREENLEAF WHITTIER.

With Illustrations by

GEORGE G. WHITE, H. FENN, AND CHARLES A. BARRY.

BOSTON:
FIELDS, OSGOOD, & CO.,
SUCCESSORS TO TICKNOR AND FIELDS.
1869.

UNIVERSITY PRESS: WELCH, BIGELOW, & CO.,
CAMBRIDGE.

CONTENTS.

NOT unto us who did but seek
The word that burned within to speak,
Not unto us this day belong
The triumph and exultant song.

Upon us fell in early youth
The burden of unwelcome truth,
And left us, weak and frail and few,
The censor's painful work to do.

Thenceforth our life a fight became,
The air we breathed was hot with blame;
For not with gauged and softened tone
We made the bondman's cause our own.

We bore, as Freedom's hope forlorn,
The private hate, the public scorn;
Yet held through all the paths we trod
Our faith in man and trust in God.

We prayed and hoped; but still, with awe,
The coming of the sword we saw;
We heard the nearing steps of doom,
And saw the shade of things to come.

In grief which they alone can feel
Who from a mother's wrong appeal,

With blended lines of fear and hope
We cast our country's horoscope.

For still within her house of life
We marked the lurid sign of strife,
And, poisoning and embittering all,
We saw the star of Wormwood fall.

Deep as our love for her, became
Our hate of all that wrought her shame,
And if, thereby, with tongue and pen
We erred, — we were but mortal men.

We hoped for peace: our eyes survey
The blood-red dawn of Freedom's day;
We prayed for love to loose the chain;
'T is shorn by battle's axe in twain!

Not skill nor strength nor zeal of ours
Has mined and heaved the hostile towers;
Not by our hands is turned the key
That sets the sighing captives free.

A redder sea than Egypt's wave
Is piled and parted for the slave;
A darker cloud moves on in light,
A fiercer fire is guide by night!

The praise, O Lord! be Thine alone,
In Thy own way Thy work be done!
Our poor gifts at Thy feet we cast,
To whom be glory, first and last!

3d Mo., 1865.

NATIONAL LYRICS.

STANZAS.

OUR fellow-countrymen in chains!
  Slaves — in a land of light and law!
Slaves — crouching on the very plains
  Where rolled the storm of Freedom's war!

A groan from Eutaw's haunted wood —
  A wail where Camden's martyrs fell —
By every shrine of patriot blood,
  From Moultrie's wall and Jasper's well!

By storied hill and hallowed grot,
  By mossy wood and marshy glen,
Whence rang of old the rifle-shot,
  And hurrying shout of Marion's men!
The groan of breaking hearts is there —
  The falling lash — the fetter's clank!
Slaves — SLAVES are breathing in that air,
  Which old De Kalb and Sumter drank!

What, ho! — *our* countrymen in chains!
  The whip on WOMAN'S shrinking flesh!
Our soil yet reddening with the stains,
  Caught from her scourging, warm and fresh!
What! mothers from their children riven!
  What! God's own image bought and sold!
AMERICANS to market driven,
  And bartered as the brute for gold!

Speak! shall their agony of prayer
  Come thrilling to our hearts in vain?
To us whose fathers scorned to bear
  The paltry *menace* of a chain;
To us, whose boast is loud and long
  Of holy Liberty and Light —
Say, shall these writhing slaves of Wrong,
  Plead vainly for their plundered Right?

What! shall we send, with lavish breath,
  Our sympathies across the wave,
Where Manhood, on the field of death,
  Strikes for his freedom, or a grave?
Shall prayers go up, and hymns be sung
  For Greece, the Moslem fetter spurning,
And millions hail with pen and tongue
  Our light on all her altars burning?

Shall Belgium feel, and gallant France,
  By Vendome's pile and Schoenbrun's wall,
And Poland, gasping on her lance,
  The impulse of our cheering call?
And shall the SLAVE, beneath our eye,
  Clank o'er *our* fields his hateful chain?
And toss his fettered arms on high,
  And groan for Freedom's gift, in vain?

Oh, say, shall Prussia's banner be
  A refuge for the stricken slave?
And shall the Russian serf go free
  By Baikal's lake and Neva's wave?
And shall the wintry-bosomed Dane
  Relax the iron hand of pride,
And bid his bondmen cast the chain
  From fettered soul and limb, aside?

Shall every flap of England's flag
  Proclaim that all around are free,
From "farthest Ind" to each blue crag
  That beetles o'er the Western Sea?
And shall we scoff at Europe's kings,
  When Freedom's fire is dim with us,
And round our country's altar clings
  The damning shade of Slavery's curse?

Go — let us ask of Constantine
  To loose his grasp on Poland's throat;
And beg the lord of Mahmoud's line
  To spare the struggling Suliote —
Will not the scorching answer come
  From turbaned Turk, and scornful Russ:
"Go, loose your fettered slaves at home,
  Then turn, and ask the like of us!"

Just God! and shall we calmly rest,
  The Christian's scorn — the heathen's mirth —
Content to live the lingering jest
  And by-word of a mocking Earth?

Shall our own glorious land retain
  That curse which Europe scorns to bear?
Shall our own brethren drag the chain
  Which not even Russia's menials wear?

Up, then, in Freedom's manly part,
  From gray-beard eld to fiery youth,
And on the nation's naked heart
  Scatter the living coals of Truth!
Up — while ye slumber, deeper yet
  The shadow of our fame is growing!
Up — while ye pause, our sun may set
  In blood, around our altars flowing!

Oh! rouse ye, ere the storm comes forth —
  The gathered wrath of God and man —
Like that which wasted Egypt's earth,
  When hail and fire above it ran.
Hear ye no warnings in the air?
  Feel ye no earthquake underneath?
Up — up — why will ye slumber where
  The sleeper only wakes in death?

Up *now* for Freedom! — not in strife
  Like that your sterner fathers saw —
The awful waste of human life —
  The glory and the guilt of war:
But break the chain — the yoke remove,
  And smite to earth Oppression's rod,
With those mild arms of Truth and Love,
  Made mighty through the living God!

Down let the shrine of Moloch sink,
  And leave no traces where it stood;
Nor longer let its idol drink
  His daily cup of human blood:
But rear another altar there,
  To Truth and Love and Mercy given,
And Freedom's gift, and Freedom's prayer,
  Shall call an answer down from Heaven!

CLERICAL OPPRESSORS.

JUST God! — and these are they
Who minister at thine altar, God of Right!
Men who their hands with prayer and blessing lay
On Israel's Ark of light!

What! preach and kidnap men?
Give thanks — and rob thy own afflicted poor?
Talk of thy glorious liberty, and then
Bolt hard the captive's door?

What! servants of thy own
Merciful Son, who came to seek and save
The homeless and the outcast, — fettering down
The tasked and plundered slave!

Pilate and Herod, friends!
Chief priests and rulers, as of old, combine!
Just God and holy! is that church, which lends
Strength to the spoiler, thine?

Paid hypocrites, who turn
Judgment aside, and rob the Holy Book
Of those high words of truth which search and burn
In warning and rebuke;

Feed fat, ye locusts, feed!
And, in your tasselled pulpits, thank the Lord
That, from the toiling bondman's utter need,
Ye pile your own full board.

How long, O Lord! how long
Shall such a priesthood barter truth away,
And, in thy name, for robbery and wrong
At thy own altars pray?

Is not thy hand stretched forth
Visibly in the heavens, to awe and smite?
Shall not the living God of all the earth,
And heaven above, do right?

Woe, then, to all who grind
Their brethren of a common Father down!
To all who plunder from the immortal mind
Its bright and glorious crown!

Woe to the priesthood! woe
To those whose hire is with the price of blood —
Perverting, darkening, changing as they go,
The searching truths of God!

Their glory and their might
Shall perish; and their very names shall be
Vile before all the people, in the light
Of a world's liberty.

Oh! speed the moment on
When Wrong shall cease — and Liberty, and Love,
And Truth, and Right, throughout the earth be known
As in their home above.

THE CHRISTIAN SLAVE.

A CHRISTIAN! going, gone!
Who bids for God's own image? — for his grace
Which that poor victim of the market-place
Hath in her suffering won?

My God! can such things be?
Hast Thou not said that whatsoe'er is done
Unto thy weakest and thy humblest one,
Is even done to Thee?

In that sad victim, then,
Child of thy pitying love, I see Thee stand —
Once more the jest-word of a mocking band,
Bound, sold, and scourged again!

A Christian up for sale!
Wet with her blood your whips — o'ertask her frame,
Make her life loathsome with your wrong and shame,
Her patience shall not fail!

A heathen hand might deal
Back on your heads the gathered wrong of years,
But her low, broken prayer and nightly tears,
Ye neither heed nor feel.

Con well thy lesson o'er,
Thou *prudent* teacher — tell the toiling slave
No dangerous tale of Him who came to save
The outcast and the poor.

But wisely shut the ray
Of God's free Gospel from her simple heart,
And to her darkened mind alone impart
One stern command — OBEY!

So shalt thou deftly raise
The market price of human flesh; and while
On thee, their pampered guest, the planters smile,
Thy church shall praise.

Grave, reverend men shall tell
From Northern pulpits how thy work was blest,
While in that vile South Sodom, first and best,
Thy poor disciples sell.

Oh, shame! the Moslem thrall,
Who, with his master, to the Prophet kneels,
While turning to the sacred Kebla feels
His fetters break and fall.

Cheers for the turbaned Bey
Of robber-peopled Tunis! he hath torn
The dark slave-dungeons open, and hath borne
Their inmates into day:

But our poor slave in vain
Turns to the Christian shrine his aching eyes —
Its rites will only swell his market price,
And rivet on his chain.

God of all right! how long
Shall priestly robbers at thine altar stand,
Lifting in prayer to Thee, the bloody hand
And haughty brow of wrong?

Oh, from the fields of cane,
From the low rice-swamp, from the trader's cell —
From the black slave-ship's foul and loathsome hell,
And coffle's weary chain, —

Hoarse, horrible, and strong,
Rises to Heaven that agonizing cry,
Filling the arches of the hollow sky,
How LONG, O GOD, HOW LONG?

STANZAS FOR THE TIMES.

IS this the land our fathers loved,
  The freedom which they toiled to win?
Is this the soil whereon they moved?
  Are these the graves they slumber in?
Are *we* the sons by whom are borne
The mantles which the dead have worn?

And shall we crouch above these graves,
  With craven soul and fettered lip?
Yoke in with marked and branded slaves,
  And tremble at the driver's whip?
Bend to the earth our pliant knees,
And speak — but as our masters please?

Shall outraged Nature cease to feel?
  Shall Mercy's tears no longer flow?
Shall ruffian threats of cord and steel —
  The dungeon's gloom — the assassin's blow,
Turn back the spirit roused to save
The Truth, our Country, and the Slave?

Of human skulls that shrine was made,
  Round which the priests of Mexico
Before their loathsome idol prayed, —
  Is Freedom's altar fashioned so?
And must we yield to Freedom's God,
As offering meet, the negro's blood?

Shall tongues be mute, when deeds are wrought
  Which well might shame extremest hell?
Shall freemen lock the indignant thought?
  Shall Pity's bosom cease to swell?
Shall Honor bleed? — Shall Truth succumb?
Shall pen, and press, and soul be dumb?

No — by each spot of haunted ground,
  Where Freedom weeps her children's fall —
By Plymouth's rock, and Bunker's mound —
  By Griswold's stained and shattered wall —
By Warren's ghost — by Langdon's shade —
By all the memories of our dead!

By their enlarging souls, which burst
  The bands and fetters round them set —
By the free Pilgrim spirit nursed
  Within our inmost bosoms, yet —
By all above — around — below —
Be ours the indignant answer — NO!

No — guided by our country's laws,
  For truth, and right, and suffering man,
Be ours to strive in Freedom's cause,
  As Christians *may* — as freemen *can!*
Still pouring on unwilling ears
That truth oppression only fears.

What! shall we guard our neighbor still,
  While woman shrieks beneath his rod,
And while he tramples down at will
  The image of a common God!
Shall watch and ward be round him set,
Of Northern nerve and bayonet?

And shall we know and share with him
  The danger and the growing shame?
And see our Freedom's light grow dim,
  Which should have filled the world with flame?
And, writhing, feel, where'er we turn,
A world's reproach around us burn?

Is 't not enough that this is borne?
  And asks our haughty neighbor more?
Must fetters which his slaves have worn,
  Clank round the Yankee farmer's door?
Must he be told, beside his plough,
What he must speak, and when, and how?

Must he be told his freedom stands
  On Slavery's dark foundations strong —
On breaking hearts and fettered hands,
  On robbery, and crime, and wrong?
That all his fathers taught is vain —
That Freedom's emblem is the chain?

Its life — its soul, from slavery drawn?
  False — foul — profane! Go — teach as well
Of holy Truth from Falsehood born!
  Of Heaven refreshed by airs from Hell!
Of Virtue in the arms of Vice!
Of Demons planting Paradise!

Rail on, then, "brethren of the South" —
  Ye shall not hear the truth the less —
No seal is on the Yankee's mouth,
  No fetter on the Yankee's press!
From our Green Mountains to the Sea,
One voice shall thunder — WE ARE FREE!

THE FAREWELL

OF A VIRGINIA SLAVE MOTHER TO HER DAUGHTERS SOLD INTO SOUTHERN BONDAGE.

GONE, gone — sold and gone,
To the rice-swamp dank and lone.
Where the slave-whip ceaseless swings,
Where the noisome insect stings,

Where the fever demon strews
Poison with the falling dews,
Where the sickly sunbeams glare
Through the hot and misty air, —
Gone, gone — sold and gone,
To the rice-swamp dank and lone,
From Virginia's hills and waters, —
Woe is me, my stolen daughters!

Gone, gone — sold and gone,
To the rice-swamp dank and lone.
There no mother's eye is near them,
There no mother's ear can hear them;
Never, when the torturing lash
Seams their back with many a gash,
Shall a mother's kindness bless them,
Or a mother's arms caress them.
Gone, gone — sold and gone,
To the rice-swamp dank and lone,
From Virginia's hills and waters, —
Woe is me, my stolen daughters!

Gone, gone — sold and gone,
To the rice-swamp dank and lone.
Oh, when weary, sad, and slow,
From the fields at night they go,
aint with toil, and racked with pain,
To their cheerless homes again —
There no brother's voice shall greet them —
There no father's welcome meet them.
Gone, gone — sold and gone,
To the rice-swamp dank and lone,
From Virginia's hills and waters, —
Woe is me, my stolen daughters!

Gone, gone — sold and gone,
To the rice-swamp dank and lone,
From the tree whose shadow lay
On their childhood's place of play —

From the cool spring where they drank —
Rock, and hill, and rivulet bank —
From the solemn house of prayer,
And the holy counsels there, —
Gone, gone — sold and gone,
To the rice-swamp dank and lone,
From Virginia's hills and waters, —
Woe is me, my stolen daughters!

Gone, gone — sold and gone,
To the rice-swamp dank and lone.
Toiling through the weary day,
And at night the spoiler's prey.
Oh, that they had earlier died,
Sleeping calmly, side by side,
Where the tyrant's power is o'er,
And the fetter galls no more!
Gone, gone — sold and gone,
To the rice-swamp dank and lone,
From Virginia's hills and waters, —
Woe is me, my stolen daughters!

Gone, gone — sold and gone,
To the rice-swamp dank and lone.
By the holy love He beareth —
By the bruised reed He spareth —
Oh, may He, to whom alone
All their cruel wrongs are known,
Still their hope and refuge prove,
With a more than mother's love.
Gone, gone — sold and gone,
To the rice-swamp dank and lone,
From Virginia's hills and waters, —
Woe is me, my stolen daughters!

LINES,

WRITTEN ON READING THE MESSAGE OF GOVERNOR RITNER, OF PENNSYLVANIA, 1836.

THANK God for the token! — one lip is still free —
One spirit untrammelled — unbending one knee!
Like the oak of the mountain, deep-rooted and firm,
Erect, when the multitude bends to the storm;
When traitors to Freedom, and Honor, and God,
Are bowed at an Idol polluted with blood;
When the recreant North has forgotten her trust,
And the lip of her honor is low in the dust, —
Thank God, that one arm from the shackle has broken!
Thank God, that one man, as a *freeman* has spoken!

O'er thy crags, Alleghany, a blast has been blown!
Down thy tide, Susquehanna, the murmur has gone!
To the land of the South — of the charter and chain —
Of Liberty sweetened with Slavery's pain;
Where the cant of Democracy dwells on the lips
Of the forgers of fetters, and wielders of whips!
Where "chivalric" honor means really no more
Than scourging of women, and robbing the poor!
Where the Moloch of Slavery sitteth on high,
And the words which he utters are — WORSHIP, OR DIE!

Right onward, oh, speed it! Wherever the blood
Of the wronged and the guiltless is crying to God;
Wherever a slave in his fetters is pining;
Wherever the lash of the driver is twining;
Wherever from kindred, torn rudely apart,
Comes the sorrowful wail of the broken of heart;
Wherever the shackles of tyranny bind,
In silence and darkness, the God-given mind;
There, God speed it onward! — its truth will be felt —
The bonds shall be loosened — the iron shall melt!

And oh, will the land where the free soul of PENN
Still lingers and breathes over mountain and glen —
Will the land where a BENEZET'S spirit went forth
To the peeled, and the meted, and outcast of Earth —
Where the words of the Charter of Liberty first
From the soul of the sage and the patriot burst —
Where first for the wronged and the weak of their kind,
The Christian and statesman their efforts combined —
Will that land of the free and the good wear a chain ?
Will the call to the rescue of Freedom be vain ?

No, RITNER ! — her "Friends," at thy warning shall stand
Erect for the truth, like their ancestral band ;
Forgetting the feuds and the strife of past time,
Counting coldness injustice, and silence a crime ;
Turning back from the cavil of creeds, to unite
Once again for the poor in defence of the Right ;
Breasting calmly, but firmly, the full tide of Wrong,
Overwhelmed, but not borne on its surges along ;
Unappalled by the danger, the shame and the pain,
And counting each trial for Truth as their gain !

And that bold-hearted yeomanry, honest and true,
Who, haters of fraud, give to labor its due ;
Whose fathers, of old, sang in concert with thine,
On the banks of Swetara, the songs of the Rhine —
The German-born pilgrims, who first dared to brave
The scorn of the proud in the cause of the slave : —
Will the sons of such men yield the lords of the South
One brow for the brand — for the padlock one mouth ?
They cater to tyrants ? — They rivet the chain,
Which their fathers smote off, on the negro again ?

No, never ! — one voice, like the sound in the cloud,
When the roar of the storm waxes loud and more loud,
Wherever the foot of the freeman hath pressed
From the Delaware's marge to the Lake of the West,
On the South-going breezes shall deepen and grow
Till the land it sweeps over shall tremble below !

The voice of a PEOPLE — uprisen — awake —
Pennsylvania's watchword, with Freedom at stake,
Thrilling up from each valley, flung down from each height,
"OUR COUNTRY AND LIBERTY! — GOD FOR THE RIGHT!"

MASSACHUSETTS TO VIRGINIA.

THE blast from Freedom's Northern hills, upon its Southern way,
Bears greeting to Virginia from Massachusetts Bay: —
No word of haughty challenging, nor battle bugle's peal,
Nor steady tread of marching files, nor clang of horsemen's steel.

No trains of deep-mouthed cannon along our highways go —
Around our silent arsenals untrodden lies the snow;
And to the land-breeze of our ports, upon their errands far,
A thousand sails of commerce swell, but none are spread for war.

We hear thy threats, Virginia! thy stormy words and high,
Swell harshly on the Southern winds which melt along our sky;
Yet, not one brown, hard hand foregoes its honest labor here —
No hewer of our mountain oaks suspends his axe in fear.

Wild are the waves which lash the reefs along St. George's bank —
Cold on the shore of Labrador the fog lies white and dank;
Through storm and wave, and blinding mist, stout are the hearts which man
The fishing-smacks of Marblehead, the sea-boats of Cape Ann.

The cold north light and wintry sun glare on their icy forms,
Bent grimly o'er their straining lines or wrestling with the storms;
Free as the winds they drive before, rough as the waves they roam,
They laugh to scorn the slaver's threat against their rocky home.

What means the Old Dominion? Hath she forgot the day
When o'er her conquered valleys swept the Briton's steel array?
How side by side, with sons of hers, the Massachusetts men
Encountered Tarleton's charge of fire, and stout Cornwallis, then?

Forgets she how the Bay State, in answer to the call
Of her old House of Burgesses, spoke out from Faneuil Hall?
When, echoing back her Henry's cry, came pulsing on each breath
Of Northern winds, the thrilling sounds of "LIBERTY OR DEATH!"

What asks the Old Dominion? If now her sons have proved
False to their fathers' memory — false to the faith they loved,
If she can scoff at Freedom, and its great charter spurn,
Must we of Massachusetts from truth and duty turn?

We hunt your bondmen, flying from Slavery's hateful hell —
Our voices, at your bidding, take up the bloodhound's yell —
We gather, at your summons, above our fathers' graves,
From Freedom's holy altar-horns to tear your wretched slaves!

Thank God! not yet so vilely can Massachusetts bow;
The spirit of her early time is with her even now;
Dream not because her Pilgrim blood moves slow, and calm, and cool,
She thus can stoop her chainless neck, a sister's slave and tool!

All that a *sister* State should do, all that a *free* State may,
Heart, hand, and purse we proffer, as in our early day;
But that one dark loathsome burden ye must stagger with alone,
And reap the bitter harvest which ye yourselves have sown!

Hold, while ye may, your struggling slaves, and burden God's free air
With woman's shriek beneath the lash, and manhood's wild despair;
Cling closer to the "cleaving curse" that writes upon your plains
The blasting of Almighty wrath against a land of chains.

Still shame your gallant ancestry, the cavaliers of old,
By watching round the shambles where human flesh is sold —
Gloat o'er the new-born child, and count his market value, when
The maddened mother's cry of woe shall pierce the slaver's den!

Lower than plummet soundeth, sink the Virginian name;
Plant, if ye will, your fathers' graves with rankest weeds of shame;
Be, if ye will, the scandal of God's fair universe —
We wash our hands forever, of your sin, and shame, and curse.

A voice from lips whereon the coal from Freedom's shrine hath been,
Thrilled, as but yesterday, the hearts of Berkshire's mountain men:
The echoes of that solemn voice are sadly lingering still
In all our sunny valleys, on every wind-swept hill.

And when the prowling man-thief came hunting for his prey
Beneath the very shadow of Bunker's shaft of gray,
How, through the free lips of the son, the father's warning spoke;
How, from its bonds of trade and sect, the Pilgrim city broke!

A hundred thousand right arms were lifted up on high, —
A hundred thousand voices sent back their loud reply;
Through the thronged towns of Essex the startling summons rang,
And up from bench and loom and wheel her young mechanics sprang!

The voice of free, broad Middlesex — of thousands as of one —
The shaft of Bunker calling to that of Lexington —
From Norfolk's ancient villages; from Plymouth's rocky bound
To where Nantucket feels the arms of ocean close her round; —

From rich and rural Worcester, where through the calm repose
Of cultured vales and fringing woods the gentle Nashua flows,
To where Wachuset's wintry blasts the mountain larches stir,
Swelled up to Heaven the thrilling cry of "God save Latimer!"

And sandy Barnstable rose up, wet with the salt sea spray —
And Bristol sent her answering shout down Narragansett Bay !
Along the broad Connecticut old Hampden felt the thrill,
And the cheer of Hampshire's woodmen swept down from Holyoke
Hill.

The voice of Massachusetts ! Of her free sons and daughters —
Deep calling unto deep aloud — the sound of many waters !
Against the burden of that voice what tyrant power shall stand ?
No fetters in the Bay State! No slave upon her land!

Look to it well, Virginians ! In calmness we have borne,
In answer to our faith and trust, your insult and your scorn ;
You 've spurned our kindest counsels — you 've hunted for our
lives —
And shaken round our hearths and homes your manacles and
gyves !

We wage no war — we lift no arm — we fling no torch within
The fire-damps of the quaking mine beneath your soil of sin ;
We leave ye with your bondmen, to wrestle, while ye can,
With the strong upward tendencies and God-like soul of man !

But for us and for our children, the vow which we have given
For freedom and humanity, is registered in Heaven ;
No slave-hunt in our borders — no pirate on our strand!
No fetters in the Bay State — no slave upon our land!

THE BRANDED HAND.

1846.

WELCOME home again, brave seaman! with thy thoughtful brow and gray,
And the old heroic spirit of our earlier, better day, —
With that front of calm endurance, on whose steady nerve, in vain
Pressed the iron of the prison, smote the fiery shafts of pain!

Is the tyrant's brand upon thee? Did the brutal cravens aim
To make God's truth thy falsehood, his holiest work thy shame?
When, all blood-quenched, from the torture the iron was withdrawn,
How laughed their evil angel the baffled fools to scorn!

They change to wrong, the duty which God hath written out
On the great heart of humanity too legible for doubt!
They, the loathsome moral lepers, blotched from footsole up to crown,
Give to shame what God hath given unto honor and renown!

Why, that brand is highest honor! — than its traces never yet
Upon old armorial hatchments was a prouder blazon set;
And thy unborn generations, as they tread our rocky strand,
Shall tell with pride the story of their father's BRANDED HAND!

As the Templar home was welcome, bearing back from Syrian wars
The scars of Arab lances, and of Paynim scimetars,
The pallor of the prison and the shackle's crimson span,
So we meet thee, so we greet thee, truest friend of God and man!

He suffered for the ransom of the dear Redeemer's grave,
Thou for his living presence in the bound and bleeding slave;
He for a soil no longer by the feet of angels trod,
Thou for the true Shechinah, the present home of God!

For, while the jurist sitting with the slave-whip o'er him swung,
From the tortured truths of freedom the lie of slavery wrung,
And the solemn priest to Moloch, on each God-deserted shrine,
Broke the bondman's heart for bread, poured the bondman's blood
for wine, —

While the multitude in blindness to a far-off Saviour knelt,
And spurned, the while, the temple where a present Saviour dwelt;
Thou beheld'st Him in the task-field, in the prison-shadows dim,
And thy mercy to the bondman, it was mercy unto Him!

In thy lone and long night-watches, sky above and wave below,
Thou did'st learn a higher wisdom than the babbling schoolmen
know;
God's stars and silence taught thee, as his angels only can,
That the one, sole sacred thing beneath the cope of heaven, is Man!

That he who treads profanely on the scrolls of law and creed,
In the depth of God's great goodness may find mercy in his need;
But woe to him who crushes the SOUL with chain and rod,
And herds with lower natures the awful form of God!

Then lift that manly right hand, bold ploughman of the wave!
Its branded palm shall prophesy, "SALVATION TO THE SLAVE!"
Hold up its fire-wrought language, that whoso reads may feel
His heart swell strong within him, his sinews change to steel.

Hold it up before our sunshine, up against our Northern air, —
Ho! men of Massachusetts, for the love of God look there!
Take it henceforth for your standard, — like the Bruce's heart of
yore,
In the dark strife closing round ye, let that hand be seen before!

And the tyrants of the slave-land shall tremble at that sign,
When it points its finger Southward along the Puritan line:
Woe to the State-gorged leeches, and the Church's locust band,
When they look from slavery's ramparts on the coming of that
hand!

TEXAS.

VOICE OF NEW ENGLAND.

UP the hill-side, down the glen,
Rouse the sleeping citizen;
Summon out the might of men!

Like a lion growling low —
Like a night-storm rising slow —
Like the tread of unseen foe —

It is coming — it is nigh!
Stand your homes and altars by;
On your own free thresholds die.

Clang the bells in all your spires;
On the gray hills of your sires
Fling to heaven your signal-fires.

From Wachuset, lone and bleak,
Unto Berkshire's tallest peak,
Let the flame-tongued heralds speak.

O, for God and duty stand,
Heart to heart and hand to hand,
Round the old graves of the land.

Whoso shrinks or falters now,
Whoso to the yoke would bow,
Brand the craven on his brow!

Freedom's soil hath only place
For a free and fearless race —
None for traitors false and base.

Perish party — perish clan;
Strike together while ye can,
Like the arm of one strong man.

Like that angel's voice sublime,
Heard above a world of crime.
Crying of the end of time —

With one heart and with one mouth,
Let the North unto the South
Speak the word befitting both:

"What though Issachar be strong!
Ye may load his back with wrong
Overmuch and over long:

Patience with her cup o'errun,
With her weary thread outspun,
Murmurs that her work is done.

Make our Union-bond a chain,
Weak as tow in Freedom's strain
Link by link shall snap in twain.

Vainly shall your sand-wrought rope
Bind the starry cluster up,
Shattered over heaven's blue cope!

Give us bright though broken rays,
Rather than eternal haze,
Clouding o'er the full-orbed blaze.

Take your land of sun and bloom;
Only leave to Freedom room
For her plough, and forge, and loom;

Take your slavery-blackened vales;
Leave us but our own free gales,
Blowing on our thousand sails.

Boldly, or with treacherous art,
Strike the blood-wrought chain apart;
Break the Union's mighty heart;

Work the ruin, if ye will;
Pluck upon your heads an ill
Which shall grow and deepen still.

With your bondman's right arm bare,
With his heart of black despair,
Stand alone, if stand ye dare!

Onward with your fell design;
Dig the gulf and draw the line:
Fire beneath your feet the mine:

Deeply, when the wide abyss
Yawns between your land and this,
Shall ye feel your helplessness.

By the hearth, and in the bed,
Shaken by a look or tread,
Ye shall own a guilty dread.

And the curse of unpaid toil,
Downward through your generous soil
Like a fire shall burn and spoil.

Our bleak hills shall bud and blow,
Vines our rocks shall overgrow,
Plenty in our valleys flow; —

And when vengeance clouds your skies,
Hither shall ye turn your eyes,
As the lost on Paradise!

We but ask our rocky strand,
Freedom's true and brother band,
Freedom's strong and honest hand, —

Valleys by the slave untrod,
And the Pilgrim's mountain sod,
Blessed of our fathers' God!"

TO FANEUIL HALL.

1844.

MEN! — if manhood still ye claim,
  If the Northern pulse can thrill,
Roused by wrong or stung by shame,
  Freely, strongly still: —
Let the sounds of traffic die:
  Shut the mill-gate — leave the stall —
Fling the axe and hammer by —
  Throng to Faneuil Hall!

Wrongs which freemen never brooked —
  Dangers grim and fierce as they,
Which, like couching lions, looked
  On your father's way; —
These your instant zeal demand,
  Shaking with their earthquake-call
Every rood of Pilgrim land —
  Ho, to Faneuil Hall!

From your capes and sandy bars —
  From your mountain-ridges cold,
Through whose pines the westering stars
  Stoop their crowns of gold —
Come, and with your footsteps wake
  Echoes from that holy wall:
Once again, for Freedom's sake,
  Rock your fathers' hall!

Up, and tread beneath your feet
  Every cord by party spun;
Let your hearts together beat
  As the heart of one.

Banks and tariffs, stocks and trade,
Let them rise or let them fall:
Freedom asks your common aid —
Up, to Faneuil Hall!

Up, and let each voice that speaks
Ring from thence to Southern plains,
Sharply as the blow which breaks
Prison-bolts and chains!
Speak as well becomes the free —
Dreaded more than steel or ball,
Shall your calmest utterance be,
Heard from Faneuil Hall!

Have they wronged us? Let us then
Render back nor threats nor prayers;
Have they chained our free-born men?
LET US UNCHAIN THEIRS!
Up! your banner leads the van,
Blazoned "Liberty for all!"
Finish what your sires began —
Up, to Faneuil Hall!

THE PINE-TREE.

1846.

LIFT again the stately emblem on the Bay State's rusted shield,
Give to Northern winds the Pine-Tree on our banner's tattered field,
Sons of men who sat in council with their Bibles round the board,
Answering England's royal missive with a firm, "THUS SAITH THE LORD!"
Rise again for home and freedom! — set the battle in array! —
What the fathers did of old time we their sons must do to-day.

Tell us not of banks and tariffs — cease your paltry peddler cries —
Shall the good State sink her honor that your gambling stocks may rise?
Would ye barter man for cotton? — That your gains may sum up higher,
Must we kiss the feet of Moloch, pass our children through the fire?
Is the dollar only real? — God and truth and right a dream?
Weighed against your lying ledgers must our manhood kick the beam?

O my God! — for that free spirit, which of old in Boston town
Smote the Province House with terror, struck the crest of Andros down! —
For another strong-voiced Adams in the city's streets to cry:
"Up for God and Massachusetts! — Set your feet on Mammon's lie!
Perish banks and perish traffic — spin your cotton's latest pound —
But in Heaven's name keep your honor — keep the heart o' the Bay State sound!"

Where 's the MAN for Massachusetts? — Where 's the voice to speak her free? —
Where 's the hand to light up bonfires from her mountains to the sea?
Beats her Pilgrim pulse no longer? — Sits she dumb in her despair? —
Has she none to break the silence? — Has she none to do and dare?
O my God! for one right worthy to lift up her rusted shield,
And to plant again the Pine-Tree in her banner's tattered field!

LINES,

SUGGESTED BY A VISIT TO THE CITY OF WASHINGTON IN THE 12TH MONTH OF 1845.

WITH a cold and wintry noon-light,
On its roofs and steeples shed,
Shadows weaving with the sunlight
From the gray sky overhead,
Broadly, vaguely, all around me, lies the half-built town outspread.

Through this broad street, restless ever,
Ebbs and flows a human tide,
Wave on wave a living river;
Wealth and fashion side by side;
Toiler, idler, slave and master, in the same quick current glide.

Underneath yon dome, whose coping
Springs above them, vast and tall,
Grave men in the dust are groping
For the largess, base and small,
Which the hand of Power is scattering, crumbs which from its table fall.

Base of heart! They vilely barter
Honor's wealth for party's place:
Step by step on Freedom's charter
Leaving footprints of disgrace;
For to-day's poor pittance turning from the great hope of their race.

Yet, where festal lamps are throwing
Glory round the dancer's hair,
Gold-tressed, like an angel's flowing
Backward on the sunset air;
And the low quick pulse of music beats its measures sweet and rare:

There to-night shall woman's glances,
Star-like, welcome give to them,
Fawning fools with shy advances
Seek to touch their garments' hem,
With the tongue of flattery glozing deeds which God and Truth condemn.

From this glittering lie my vision
Takes a broader, sadder range,
Full before me have arisen
Other pictures dark and strange;
From the parlor to the prison must the scene and witness change.

Hark! the heavy gate is swinging
On its hinges, harsh and slow;
One pale prison lamp is flinging
On a fearful group below
Such a light as leaves to terror whatsoe'er it does not show.

Pitying God! — Is that a WOMAN
On whose wrist the shackles clash?
Is that shriek she utters human,
Underneath the stinging lash?
Are they MEN whose eyes of madness from that sad procession flash?

Still the dance goes gayly onward!
What is it to Wealth and Pride?
That without the stars are looking
On a scene which earth should hide?
That the SLAVE-SHIP lies in waiting, rocking on Potomac's tide!

Vainly to that mean Ambition
Which, upon a rival's fall,
Winds above its old condition,
With a reptile's slimy crawl,
Shall the pleading voice of sorrow, shall the slave in anguish call?

Vainly to the child of Fashion,
Giving to ideal woe
Graceful luxury of compassion,
Shall the stricken mourner go;
Hateful seems the earnest sorrow, beautiful the hollow show!

Nay, my words are all too sweeping;
In this crowded human mart,
Feeling is not dead, but sleeping;
Man's strong will and woman's heart,
In the coming strife for Freedom, yet shall bear their generous part.

And from yonder sunny valleys,
Southward in the distance lost,
Freedom yet shall summon allies
Worthier than the North can boast,
With the Evil by their hearth-stones grappling at severer cost.

Now, the soul alone is willing.
Faint the heart and weak the knee;
And as yet no lip is thrilling
With the mighty words "BE FREE!"
Tarrieth long the land's Good Angel, but his advent is to be!

Meanwhile, turning from the revel
To the prison-cell my sight,
For intenser hate of evil,
For a keener sense of right,
Shaking off thy dust, I thank thee, City of the Slaves, to-night!

"To thy duty now and ever!
Dream no more of rest or stay;
Give to Freedom's great endeavor
All thou art and hast to-day": —
Thus, above the city's murmur, saith a Voice, or seems to say.

Ye with heart and vision gifted
To discern and love the right,

Whose worn faces have been lifted
  To the slowly-growing light,
Where from Freedom's sunrise drifted slowly back the murk of night! —

Ye who through long years of trial
  Still have held your purpose fast,
While a lengthening shade the dial
  From the westering sunshine cast,
And of hope each hour's denial seemed an echo of the last! —

O my brothers! O my sisters!
  Would to God that ye were near,
Gazing with me down the vistas
  Of a sorrow strange and drear;
Would to God that ye were listeners to the Voice I seem to hear!

With the storm above us driving,
  With the false earth mined below —
Who shall marvel if thus striving
  We have counted friend as foe;
Unto one another giving in the darkness blow for blow.

Well it may be that our natures
  Have grown sterner and more hard,
And the freshness of their features
  Somewhat harsh and battle-scarred,
And their harmonies of feeling overtasked and rudely jarred.

Be it so. It should not swerve us
  From a purpose true and brave;
Dearer Freedom's rugged service
  Than the pastime of the slave;
Better is the storm above it than the quiet of the grave.

Let us then, uniting, bury
  All our idle feuds in dust,
And to future conflicts carry
  Mutual faith and common trust;
Always he who most forgiveth in his brother is most just.

From the eternal shadow rounding
. All our sun and starlight here,
Voices of our lost ones sounding
Bid us be of heart and cheer,
Through the silence, down the spaces, falling on the inward ear.

Know we not our dead are looking
Downward with a sad surprise,
All our strife of words rebuking
With their mild and loving eyes?
Shall we grieve the holy angels? Shall we cloud their blessed skies?

Let us draw their mantles o'er us
Which have fallen in our way;
Let us do the work before us,
Cheerly, bravely, while we may,
Ere the long night-silence cometh, and with us it is not day!

YORKTOWN.

FROM Yorktown's ruins, ranked and still,
Two lines stretch far o'er vale and hill:
Who curbs his steed at head of one?
Hark! the low murmur: Washington!
Who bends his keen, approving glance
Where down the gorgeous line of France
Shine knightly star and plume of snow?
Thou too art victor, Rochambeau!

The earth which bears this calm array
Shook with the war-charge yesterday,
Ploughed deep with hurrying hoof and wheel,
Shot-sown and bladed thick with steel;

October's clear and noonday sun
Paled in the breath-smoke of the gun,
And down night's double blackness fell,
Like a dropped star, the blazing shell.

Now all is hushed: the gleaming lines
Stand moveless as the neighboring pines;
While through them, sullen, grim, and slow,
The conquered hosts of England go:
O'Hara's brow belies his dress,
Gay Tarleton's troop rides bannerless:
Shout, from thy fired and wasted homes,
Thy scourge, Virginia, captive comes!

Nor thou alone: with one glad voice
Let all thy sister States rejoice;
Let Freedom, in whatever clime
She waits with sleepless eye her time,
Shouting from cave and mountain wood,
Make glad her desert solitude,
While they who hunt her quail with fear:
The New World's chain lies broken here!

But who are they, who, cowering, wait
Within the shattered fortress gate?
Dark tillers of Virginia's soil,
Classed with the battle's common spoil,
With household stuffs, and fowl, and swine,
With Indian weed and planters' wine,
With stolen beeves, and foraged corn, —
Are they not men, Virginian born?

O, veil your faces, young and brave!
Sleep, Scammel, in thy soldier grave!
Sons of the Northland, ye who set
Stout hearts against the bayonet,
And pressed with steady foötfall near
The moated battery's blazing tier,
Turn your scarred faces from the sight,
Let shame do homage to the right!

Lo! threescore years have passed; and where
The Gallic timbrel stirred the air,
With Northern drum-roll, and the clear,
Wild horn-blow of the mountaineer,
While Britain grounded on that plain
The arms she might not lift again,
As abject as in that old day
The slave still toils his life away.

O, fields still green and fresh in story,
Old days of pride, old names of glory,
Old marvels of the tongue and pen,
Old thoughts which stirred the hearts of men,
Ye spared the wrong; and over all
Behold the avenging shadow fall!
Your world-wide honor stained with shame, —
Your freedom's self a hollow name!

Where 's now the flag of that old war?
Where flows its stripe? Where burns its star?
Bear witness, Palo Alto's day,
Dark Vale of Palms, red Monterey,
Where Mexic Freedom, young and weak,
Fleshes the Northern eagle's beak:
Symbol of terror and despair,
Of chains and slaves, go seek it there!

Laugh, Prussia, midst thy iron ranks!
Laugh, Russia, from thy Neva's banks!
Brave sport to see the fledgling born
Of Freedom by its parent torn!
Safe now is Speilberg's dungeon cell,
Safe drear Siberia's frozen hell:
With Slavery's flag o'er both unrolled,
What of the New World fears the Old?

THE WATCHERS.

BESIDE a stricken field I stood;
On the torn turf, on grass and wood,
Hung heavily the dew of blood.

Still in their fresh mounds lay the slain,
But all the air was quick with pain
And gusty sighs and tearful rain.

Two angels, each with drooping head
And folded wings and noiseless tread,
Watched by that valley of the dead.

The one, with forehead saintly bland
And lips of blessing, not command,
Leaned, weeping, on her olive wand.

The other's brows were scarred and knit,
His restless eyes were watch-fires lit,
His hands for battle-gauntlets fit.

"How long!" — I knew the voice of Peace, —
"Is there no respite? — no release? —
When shall the hopeless quarrel cease?

"O Lord, how long! — One human soul
Is more than any parchment scroll,
Or any flag thy winds unroll.

"What price was Ellsworth's, young and brave?
How weigh the gift that Lyon gave,
Or count the cost of Winthrop's grave?

"O brother! if thine eye can see,
Tell how and when the end shall be,
What hope remains for thee and me."

Then Freedom sternly said: "I shun
No strife nor pang beneath the sun,
When human rights are staked and won.

"I knelt with Ziska's hunted flock,
I watched in Toussaint's cell of rock,
I walked with Sidney to the block.

"The moor of Marston felt my tread,
Through Jersey snows the march I led,
My voice Magenta's charges sped.

"But now, through weary day and night,
I watch a vague and aimless fight
For leave to strike one blow aright.

"On either side my foe they own:
One guards through love his ghastly throne,
And one through fear to reverence grown.

"Why wait we longer, mocked, betrayed,
By open foes, or those afraid
To speed thy coming through my aid?

"Why watch to see who win or fall? —
I shake the dust against them all,
I leave them to their senseless brawl."

"Nay," Peace implored: "yet longer wait;
The doom is near, the stake is great:
God knoweth if it be too late.

"Still wait and watch; the way prepare
Where I with folded wings of prayer
May follow, weaponless and bare."

"Too late!" the stern, sad voice replied,
"Too late!" its mournful echo sighed,
In low lament the answer died.

A rustling as of wings in flight,
An upward gleam of lessening white,
So passed the vision, sound and sight.

But round me, like a silver bell
Rung down the listening sky to tell
Of holy help, a sweet voice fell.

"Still hope and trust," it sang; "the rod
Must fall, the wine-press must be trod,
But all is possible with God!"

LINES,

WRITTEN ON THE ADOPTION OF PINCKNEY'S RESOLUTIONS, IN THE HOUSE OF REPRESENTATIVES, AND THE PASSAGE OF CALHOUN'S "BILL FOR EXCLUDING PAPERS, WRITTEN OR PRINTED, TOUCHING THE SUBJECT OF SLAVERY FROM THE U. S. POST-OFFICE," IN THE SENATE OF THE UNITED STATES.

MEN of the North-land! where 's the manly spirit
Of the true-hearted and the unshackled gone?
Sons of old freemen, do we but inherit
Their names alone?

Is the old Pilgrim spirit quenched within us,
Stoops the strong manhood of our souls so low,
That Mammon's lure or Party's wile can win us
To silence now!

Now, when our land to ruin's brink is verging,
In God's name, let us speak while there is time!
Now, when the padlocks for our lips are forging,
Silence is crime!

What! shall we henceforth humbly ask as favors
Rights all our own? In madness shall we barter,
For treacherous peace, the freedom Nature gave us,
God and our charter?

Here shall the statesman forge his human fetters,
Here the false jurist human rights deny,
And, in the church, their proud and skilled abettors
Make truth a lie?

Torture the pages of the hallowed Bible,
To sanction crime, and robbery, and blood?
And, in Oppression's hateful service, libel
Both man and God?

Shall our New England stand erect no longer,
  But stoop in chains upon her downward way,
Thicker to gather on her limbs and stronger
                    Day after day?

O no; methinks from all her wild, green mountains —
  From valleys where her slumbering fathers lie —
From her blue rivers and her welling fountains,
                    And clear, cold sky —

From her rough coast, and isles, which hungry Ocean
  Gnaws with his surges — from the fisher's skiff,
With white sail swaying to the billows' motion
                    Round rock and cliff —

From the free fireside of her unbought farmer —
  From her free laborer at his loom and wheel —
From the brown smith-shop, where, beneath the hammer,
                    Rings the red steel —

From each and all, if God hath not forsaken
  Our land, and left us to an evil choice,
Loud as the summer thunderbolt shall waken
                    A People's voice

Startling and stern! the Northern winds shall bear it
  Over Potomac's to St. Mary's wave;
And buried Freedom shall awake to hear it
                    Within her grave.

O, let that voice go forth! The bondman sighing
  By Santee's wave, in Mississippi's cane,
Shall feel the hope, within his bosom dying,
                    Revive again.

Let it go forth! The millions who are gazing
  Sadly upon us from afar, shall smile,
And unto God devout thanksgiving raising,
                    Bless us the while.

O, for your ancient freedom, pure and holy,
  For the deliverance of a groaning earth,
For the wronged captive, bleeding, crushed, and lowly,
  Let it go forth!

Sons of the best of fathers! will ye falter
  With all they left ye perilled and at stake?
Ho! once again on Freedom's holy altar
  The fire awake!

Prayer-strengthened for the trial, come together,
  Put on the harness for the moral fight,
And, with the blessing of your Heavenly Father,
  MAINTAIN THE RIGHT!

THE CRISIS.

WRITTEN ON LEARNING THE TERMS OF THE TREATY WITH MEXICO.

ACROSS the Stony Mountains, o'er the desert's drouth and sand,
The circles of our empire touch the Western Ocean's strand;
From slumberous Timpanogos, to Gila, wild and free,
Flowing down from Neuva Leon to California's sea;
And from the mountains of the East, to Santa Rosa's shore,
The eagles of Mexitli shall beat the air no more.

O Vale of Rio Bravo! Let thy simple children weep;
Close watch about their holy fire let maids of Pecos keep;
Let Taos send her cry across Sierra Madre's pines,
And Algodones toll her bells amidst her corn and vines;
For lo! the pale land-seekers come, with eager eyes of gain,
Wide scattering, like the bison herds on broad Salada's plain.

Let Sacramento's herdsmen heed what sound, the winds bring down,
Of footsteps on the crisping snow, from cold Neveda's crown!
Full hot and fast the Saxon rides, with rein of travel slack,
And, bending o'er his saddle, leaves the sunrise at his back;
By many a lonely river, and gorge of fir and pine,
On many a wintry hill-top, his nightly camp-fires shine.

O countrymen and brothers! that land of lake and plain,
Of salt wastes alternating with valleys fat with grain;
Of mountains white with winter, looking downward, cold, serene,
On their feet with spring-vines tangled and lapped in softest geeen;
Swift through whose black volcanic gates, o'er many a sunny vale,
Wind-like the Arapahoe sweeps the bison's dusty trail!

Great spaces yet untravelled, great lakes whose mystic shores
The Saxon rifle never heard, nor dip of Saxon oars;
Great herds that wander all unwatched, wild steeds that none have tamed,
Strange fish in unknown streams, and birds the Saxon never named;
Deep mines, dark mountain crucibles, where Nature's chemic powers
Work out the Great Designer's will: — all these ye say are ours!

Forever ours! for good or ill, on us the burden lies;
God's balance, watched by angels, is hung across the skies.
Shall Justice, Truth, and Freedom, turn the poised and trembling scale?
Or shall the Evil triumph, and robber Wrong prevail?
Shall the broad land o'er which our flag in starry splendor waves,
Forego through us its freedom, and bear the tread of slaves?

The day is breaking in the East, of which the prophets told,
And brightens up the sky of Time the Christian Age of Gold:
Old Might to Right is yielding, battle blade to clerkly pen,
Earth's monarchs are her peoples, and her serfs stand up as men;
The isles rejoice together, in a day are nations born,
And the slave walks free in Tunis, and by Stamboul's Golden Horn!

Is this, O countrymen of mine! a day for us to sow
The soil of new-gained empire with slavery's seeds of woe?
To feed with our fresh life-blood the old world's cast-off crime,
Dropped, like some monstrous early birth, from the tired lap of
 Time?
To run anew the evil race the old lost nations ran,
And die like them of unbelief of God, and wrong of man?

Great Heaven! Is this our mission? End in this the prayers
 and tears,
The toil, the strife, the watchings of our younger, better years?
Still, as the old world rolls in light, shall ours in shadow turn,
A beamless Chaos, cursed of God, through outer darkness borne?
Where the far nations looked for light, a blackness in the air?
Where for words of hope they listened, the long wail of despair?

The Crisis presses on us; face to face with us it stands,
With solemn lips of question, like the Sphinx in Egypt's sands!
This day we fashion Destiny, our web of Fate we spin;
This day for all hereafter choose we holiness or sin;
Even now from starry Gerizim, or Ebal's cloudy crown,
We call the dews of blessing or the bolts of cursing down!

By all for which the martyrs bore their agony and shame;
By all the warning words of truth with which the prophets came;
By the Future which awaits us; by all the hopes which cast
Their faint and trembling beams across the blackness of the Past;
And by the blessed thought of Him who for Earth's freedom died,
O my people! O my brothers! let us choose the righteous side.

So shall the Northern pioneer go joyful on his way;
To wed Penobscot's waters to San Francisco's bay;
To make the rugged places smooth, and sow the vales with grain;
And bear, with Liberty and Law, the Bible in his train:
The mighty West shall bless the East, and sea shall answer sea,
And mountain unto mountain call: PRAISE GOD, FOR WE ARE
 FREE!

RANDOLPH OF ROANOKE.

O MOTHER Earth! upon thy lap
  Thy weary ones receiving,
And o'er them, silent as a dream,
  Thy grassy mantle weaving,
Fold softly in thy long embrace
  That heart so worn and broken,
And cool its pulse of fire beneath
  Thy shadows old and oaken.

Shut out from him the bitter word
  And serpent hiss of scorning;
Nor let the storms of yesterday
  Disturb his quiet morning.
Breathe over him forgetfulness
  Of all save deeds of kindness,
And, save to smiles of grateful eyes,
  Press down his lids in blindness.

There, where with living ear and eye
  He heard Potomac's flowing,
And, through his tall ancestral trees,
  Saw Autumn's sunset glowing,
He sleeps, — still looking to the West,
  Beneath the dark wood shadow,
As if he still would see the sun
  Sink down on wave and meadow.

Bard, Sage, and Tribune! — in himself
  All moods of mind contrasting, —
The tenderest wail of human woe,
  The scorn-like lightning blasting;

The pathos which from rival eyes
  Unwilling tears could summon,
The stinging taunt, the fiery burst
  Of hatred scarcely human!

Mirth, sparkling like a diamond shower,
  From lips of life-long sadness;
Clear picturings of majestic thought
  Upon a ground of madness;
And over all Romance and Song
  A classic beauty throwing,
And laurelled Clio at his side
  Her storied pages showing.

All parties feared him: each in turn
  Beheld its schemes disjointed,
As right or left his fatal glance
  And spectral finger pointed.
Sworn foe of Cant, he smote it down
  With trenchant wit unsparing,
And, mocking, rent with ruthless hand
  The robe Pretence was wearing.

Too honest or too proud to feign
  A love he never cherished,
Beyond Virginia's border line
  His patriotism perished.
While others hailed in distant skies
  Our eagle's dusky pinion,
He only saw the mountain bird
  Stoop o'er his Old Dominion!

Still through each change of fortune strange,
  Racked nerve, and brain all burning,
His loving faith in Mother-land
  Knew never shade of turning;
By Britain's lakes, by Neva's wave,
  Whatever sky was o'er him,
He heard her rivers' rushing sound,
  Her blue peaks rose before him.

He held his slaves, yet made withal
  No false and vain pretences,
Nor paid a lying priest to seek
  For scriptural defences.
His harshest words of proud rebuke,
  His bitterest taunt and scorning,
Fell fire-like on the Northern brow
  That bent to him in fawning.

He held his slaves: yet kept the while
  His reverence for the Human;
In the dark vassals of his will
  He saw but Man and Woman!
No hunter of God's outraged poor
  His Roanoke valley entered;
No trader in the souls of men
  Across his threshold ventured.

And when the old and wearied man
  Laid down for his last sleeping,
And at his side, a slave no more,
  His brother man stood weeping,
His latest thought, his latest breath,
  To Freedom's duty giving,
With failing tongue and trembling hand
  The dying blest the living.

O, never bore his ancient State
  A truer son or braver!
None trampling with a calmer scorn
  On foreign hate or favor.
He knew her faults, yet never stooped
  His proud and manly feeling
To poor excuses of the wrong
  Or meanness of concealing.

But none beheld with clearer eye
  The plague-spot o'er her spreading,
None heard more sure the steps of Doom
  Along her future treading.

For her as for himself he spake,
  When, his gaunt frame upbracing,
He traced with dying hand "REMORSE!"
  And perished in the tracing.

As from the grave where Henry sleeps,
  From Vernon's weeping willow,
And from the grassy pall which hides
  The Sage of Monticello,
So from the leaf-strewn burial-stone
  Of Randolph's lowly dwelling,
Virginia! o'er thy land of slaves
  A warning voice is swelling!

And hark! from thy deserted fields
  Are sadder warnings spoken,
From quenched hearths, where thy exiled sons
  Their household gods have broken.
The curse is on thee, — wolves for men,
  And briers for corn-sheaves giving!
O, more than all thy dead renown
  Were now one hero living!

THE ANGELS OF BUENA VISTA.

SPEAK and tell us, our Ximena, looking northward far away,
O'er the camp of the invaders, o'er the Mexican array,
Who is losing? who is winning? are they far or come they near?
Look abroad, and tell us, sister, whither rolls the storm we hear.

"Down the hills of Angostura still the storm of battle rolls;
Blood is flowing, men are dying; God have mercy on their souls!"

Who is losing? who is winning? — "Over hill and over plain,
I see but smoke of cannon clouding through the mountain rain."

Holy Mother! keep our brothers! Look, Ximena, look once more:
"Still I see the fearful whirlwind rolling darkly as before,
Bearing on, in strange confusion, friend and foeman, foot and horse,
Like some wild and troubled torrent sweeping down its mountain course."

Look forth once more, Ximena! "Ah! the smoke has rolled away;
And I see the Northern rifles gleaming down the ranks of gray.
Hark! that sudden blast of bugles! there the troop of Minon wheels;
There the Northern horses thunder, with the cannon at their heels.

"Jesu, pity! how it thickens! now retreat and now advance!
Right against the blazing cannon shivers Puebla's charging lance!
Down they go, the brave young riders; horse and foot together fall;
Like a ploughshare in the fallow, through them ploughs the Northern ball."

Nearer came the storm and nearer, rolling fast and frightful on:
Speak, Ximena, speak and tell us, who has lost, and who has won?
"Alas! alas! I know not; friend and foe together fall,
O'er the dying rush the living: pray, my sisters, for them all!"

"Lo! the wind the smoke is lifting: Blessed Mother, save my brain!
I can see the wounded crawling slowly out from heaps of slain.
Now they stagger, blind and bleeding; now they fall, and strive to rise;
Hasten, sisters, haste and save them, lest they die before our eyes!"

"O my heart's love! O my dear one! lay thy poor head on my knee;
Dost thou know the lips that kiss thee? Canst thou hear me? canst thou see?
O my husband, brave and gentle! O my Bernal, look once more
On the blessed cross before thee! mercy! mercy! all is o'er!"

Dry thy tears, my poor Ximena; lay thy dear one down to rest;
Let his hands be meekly folded, lay the cross upon his breast;
Let his dirge be sung hereafter, and his funeral masses said;
To-day, thou poor bereaved one, the living ask thy aid.

Close beside her, faintly moaning, fair and young, a soldier lay,
Torn with shot and pierced with lances, bleeding slow his life away;
But, as tenderly before him, the lorn Ximena knelt,
She saw the Northern eagle shining on his pistol-belt.

With a stifled cry of horror straight she turned away her head;
With a sad and bitter feeling looked she back upon her dead;
But she heard the youth's low moaning, and his struggling breath of pain,
And she raised the cooling water to his parching lips again.

Whispered low the dying soldier, pressed her hand and faintly smiled:
Was that pitying face his mother's? did she watch beside her child?
All his stranger words with meaning her woman's heart supplied;
With her kiss upon his forehead, "Mother!" murmured he, and died!

"A bitter curse upon them, poor boy, who led thee forth,
From some gentle, sad-eyed mother, weeping, lonely, in the North!"
Spake the mournful Mexic woman, as she laid him with her dead,
And turned to soothe the living, and bind the wounds which bled.

Look forth once more, Ximena! "Like a cloud before the wind
Rolls the battle down the mountains, leaving blood and death behind;
Ah! they plead in vain for mercy; in the dust the wounded strive;
Hide your faces, holy angels! O, thou Christ of God, forgive!"

Sink, O Night, among thy mountains! let the cool, gray shadows fall;
Dying brothers, fighting demons, drop thy curtain over all!
Through the thickening winter twilight, wide apart the battle rolled,
In its sheath the sabre rested, and the cannon's lips grew cold.

But the noble Mexic women still their holy task pursued,
Through that long, dark night of sorrow, worn and faint and lacking food;
Over weak and suffering brothers, with a tender care they hung,
And the dying foeman blessed them in a strange and Northern tongue.

Not wholly lost, O Father! is this evil world of ours;
Upward, through its blood and ashes, spring afresh the Eden flowers;
From its smoking hell of battle, Love and Pity send their prayer,
And still thy white-winged angels hover dimly in our air!

DEMOCRACY.

"All things whatsoever ye would that men should do to you, do ye even so to them." — *Matthew* vii. 12.

BEARER of Freedom's holy light,
Breaker of Slavery's chain and rod,
The foe of all which pains the sight,
Or wounds the generous ear of God!

Beautiful yet thy temples rise,
Though there profaning gifts are thrown;
And fires unkindled of the skies
Are glaring round thy altar-stone.

Still sacred, — though thy name be breathed
By those whose hearts thy truth deride;
And garlands, plucked from thee, are wreathed
Around the haughty brows of Pride.

O, ideal of my boyhood's time!
The faith in which my father stood,
Even when the sons of Lust and Crime
Had stained thy peaceful courts with blood!

Still to thōse courts my footsteps turn,
For, through the mists which darken there,
I see the flame of Freedom burn, —
The Kebla of the patriot's prayer!

The generous feeling, pure and warm,
Which owns the rights of *all* divine —
The pitying heart — the helping arm —
The prompt self-sacrifice — are thine.

Beneath thy broad, impartial eye,
How fade the lines of caste and birth!
How equal in their suffering lie
The groaning multitudes of earth!

Still to a stricken brother true,
Whatever clime hath nurtured him;
As stooped to heal the wounded Jew
The worshipper of Gerizim.

By misery unrepelled, unawed
By pomp or power, thou see'st a MAN
In prince or peasant — slave or lord —
Pale priest, or swarthy artisan.

Through all disguise, form, place, or name,
Beneath the flaunting robes of sin,
Through poverty and squalid shame,
Thou lookest on *the man* within.

On man, as man, retaining yet,
Howe'er debased, and soiled, and dim,
The crown upon his forehead set, —
The immortal gift of God to him.

And there is reverence in thy look;
 For that frail form which mortals wear
The Spirit of the Holiest took,
 And veiled his perfect brightness there.

Not from the shallow babbling fount
 Of vain philosophy thou art;
He who of old on Syria's mount
 Thrilled, warmed, by turns, the listener's heart,

In holy words which cannot die,
 In thoughts which angels leaned to know,
Proclaimed thy message from on high, —
 Thy mission to a world of woe.

That voice's echo hath not died!
 From the blue lake of Galilee,
And Tabor's lonely mountain side,
 It calls a struggling world to thee.

Thy name and watchword o'er this land
 I hear in every breeze that stirs,
And round a thousand altars stand
 Thy banded party worshippers.

Not to these altars of a day,
 At party's call, my gift I bring;
But on thy olden shrine I lay
 A freeman's dearest offering: —

The voiceless utterance of his will, —
 His pledge to Freedom and to Truth,
That manhood's heart remembers still
 The homage of his generous youth.

Election Day, 1843.

THY WILL BE DONE.

WE see not, know not; all our way
Is night, — with Thee alone is day:
From out the torrent's troubled drift,
Above the storm our prayers we lift,
Thy will be done!

The flesh may fail, the heart may faint,
But who are we to make complaint,
Or dare to plead, in times like these,
The weakness of our love of ease?
Thy will be done!

We take with solemn thankfulness
Our burden up, nor ask it less,
And count it joy that even we
May suffer, serve, or wait, for Thee,
Whose will be done!

Though dim as yet in tint and line,
We trace Thy picture's wise design,
And thank Thee that our age supplies
Its dark relief of sacrifice.
Thy will be done!

And if, in our unworthiness,
Thy sacrificial wine we press;
If from Thy ordeal's heated bars
Our feet are seamed with crimson scars,
Thy will be done!

If, for the age to come, this hour
Of trial hath vicarious power,

And, blest by Thee, our present pain
Be Liberty's eternal gain,
Thy will be done!

Strike, Thou the Master, we Thy keys,
The anthem of the destinies!
The minor of Thy loftier strain,
Our hearts shall breathe the old refrain,
Thy will be done!

"EIN FESTE BURG IST UNSER GOTT."

(LUTHER'S HYMN.)

WE wait beneath the furnace-blast
The pangs of transformation;
Not painlessly doth God recast
And mould anew the nation.
Hot burns the fire
Where wrongs expire;
Nor spares the hand
That from the land
Uproots the ancient evil.

The hand-breadth cloud the sages feared
Its bloody rain is dropping;
The poison plant the fathers spared
All else is overtopping.
East, West, South, North,
It curses the earth;
All justice dies,
And fraud and lies
Live only in its shadow.

What gives the wheat-field blades of steel?
  What points the rebel cannon?
What sets the roaring rabble's heel
  On the old star-spangled pennon?
    What breaks the oath
    Of the men o' the South?
    What whets the knife
    For the Union's life? —
  Hark to the answer: Slavery!

Then waste no blows on lesser foes
  In strife unworthy freemen.
God lifts to-day the veil, and shows
  The features of the demon!
    O North and South,
    Its victims both,
    Can ye not cry,
    "Let slavery die!"
  And union find in freedom?

What though the cast-out spirit tear
  The nation in his going?
We who have shared the guilt must share
  The pang of his o'erthrowing!
    Whate'er the loss,
    Whate'er the cross,
    Shall they complain
    Of present pain
  Who trust in God's hereafter?

For who that leans on His right arm
  Was ever yet forsaken?
What righteous cause can suffer harm
  If He its part has taken?
    Though wild and loud
    And dark the cloud,
    Behind its folds
    His hand upholds
  The calm sky of to-morrow!

Above the maddening cry for blood,
Above the wild war-drumming,
Let Freedom's voice be heard, with good
The evil overcoming.
Give prayer and purse
To stay the Curse
Whose wrong we share,
Whose shame we bear,
Whose end shall gladden Heaven!

In vain the bells of war shall ring
Of triumphs and revenges,
While still is spared the evil thing
That severs and estranges.
But blest the ear
That yet shall hear
The jubilant bell
That rings the knell
Of Slavery forever!

Then let the selfish lip be dumb,
And hushed the breath of sighing;
Before the joy of peace must come
The pains of purifying.
God give us grace
Each in his place
To bear his lot,
And, murmuring not,
Endure and wait and labor!

ASTRÆA AT THE CAPITOL.

ABOLITION OF SLAVERY IN THE DISTRICT OF COLUMBIA, 1862.

WHEN first I saw our banner wave
  Above the nation's council-hall,
  I heard beneath its marble wall
The clanking fetters of the slave!

In the foul market-place I stood,
  And saw the Christian mother sold,
  And childhood with its locks of gold,
Blue-eyed and fair with Saxon blood.

I shut my eyes, I held my breath,
  And, smothering down the wrath and shame
  That set my Northern blood aflame,
Stood silent — where to speak was death.

Beside me gloomed the prison-cell
  Where wasted one in slow decline
  For uttering simple words of mine,
And loving freedom all too well.

The flag that floated from the dome
  Flapped menace in the morning air;
  I stood a perilled stranger where
The human broker made his home.

For crime was virtue: Gown and Sword
  And Law their threefold sanction gave,
  And to the quarry of the slave
Went hawking with our symbol-bird.

On the oppressor's side was power;
  And yet I knew that every wrong,
  However old, however strong,
But waited God's avenging hour.

I knew that truth would crush the lie, —
  Somehow, sometime, the end would be;
  Yet scarcely dared I hope to see
The triumph with my mortal eye.

But now I see it! In the sun
  A free flag floats from yonder dome,
  And at the nation's hearth and home
The justice long delayed is done.

Not as we hoped, in calm of prayer,
  The message of deliverance comes,
  But heralded by roll of drums
On waves of battle-troubled air! —

Midst sounds that madden and appall,
  The song that Bethlehem's shepherds knew!
  The harp of David melting through
The demon-agonies of Saul!

Not as we hoped; — but what are we?
  Above our broken dreams and plans
  God lays, with wiser hand than man's,
The corner-stones of liberty.

I cavil not with Him: the voice
  That freedom's blessed gospel tells
  Is sweet to me as silver bells,
Rejoicing! — yea, I will rejoice!

Dear friends still toiling in the sun, —
  Ye dearer ones who, gone before,
  Are watching from the eternal shore
The slow work by your hands begun, —

Rejoice, with me! The chastening rod
  Blossoms with love; the furnace heat
  Grows cool beneath His blessed feet
Whose form is as the Son of God!

Rejoice! Our Marah's bitter springs
  Are sweetened; on our ground of grief
  Rise day by day in strong relief
The prophecies of better things.

Rejoice in hope! The day and night
  Are one with God, and one with them
  Who see by faith the cloudy hem
Of Judgment fringed with Mercy's light!

THE PASS OF THE SIERRA.

ALL night above their rocky bed
  They saw the stars march slow;
The wild Sierra overhead,
  The desert's death below.

The Indian from his lodge of bark,
  The gray bear from his den,
Beyond their camp-fire's wall of dark,
  Glared on the mountain men.

Still upward turned, with anxious strain,
  Their leader's sleepless eye,
Where splinters of the mountain chain
  Stood black against the sky.

The night waned slow: at last, a glow,
  A gleam of sudden fire,

Shot up behind the walls of snow,
  And tipped each icy spire.

"Up, men!" he cried, "yon rocky cone,
  To-day, please God, we 'll pass,
And look from Winter's frozen throne
  On Summer's flowers and grass!"

They set their faces to the blast,
  They trod th' eternal snow,
And faint, worn, bleeding, hailed at last
  The promised land below.

Behind, they saw the snow-cloud tossed
  By many an icy horn;
Before, warm valleys, wood-embossed,
  And green with vines and corn.

They left the Winter at their backs
  To flap his baffled wing,
And downward, with the cataracts,
  Leaped to the lap of Spring.

Strong leader of that mountain band
  Another task remains,
To break from Slavery's desert land
  A path to Freedom's plains.

The winds are wild, the way is drear
  Yet, flashing through the night,
Lo! icy ridge and rocky spear
  Blaze out in morning light!

Rise up, FREMONT! and go before;
  The Hour must have its Man;
Put on the hunting-shirt once more,
  And lead in Freedom's van!

8th mo., 1856.

THE BATTLE AUTUMN OF 1862.

THE flags of war like storm-birds fly,
  The charging trumpets blow;
Yet rolls no thunder in the sky,
  No earthquake strives below.

And, calm and patient, Nature keeps
  Her ancient promise well,
Though o'er her bloom and greenness sweeps
  The battle's breath of hell.

And still she walks in golden hours
  Through harvest-happy farms,
And still she wears her fruits and flowers
  Like jewels on her arms.

What mean the gladness of the plain,
  This joy of eve and morn,
The mirth that shakes the beard of grain
  And yellow locks of corn?

Ah! eyes may well be full of tears,
  And hearts with hate are hot;
But even-paced come round the years,
  And Nature changes not.

She meets with smiles our bitter grief,
  With songs our groans of pain;
She mocks with tint of flower and leaf
  The war-field's crimson stain.

Still, in the cannon's pause, we hear
  Her sweet thanksgiving-psalm;
Too near to God for doubt or fear,
  She shares th' eternal calm.

She knows the seed lies safe below
  The fires that blast and burn;
For all the tears of blood we sow
  She waits the rich return.

She sees with clearer eye than ours
  The good of suffering born, —
The hearts that blossom like her flowers,
  And ripen like her corn.

O, give to us, in times like these,
  The vision of her eyes;
And make her fields and fruited trees
  Our golden prophecies!

O, give to us her finer ear!
  Above this stormy din,
We too would hear the bells of cheer
  Ring peace and freedom in!

MITHRIDATES AT CHIOS.

KNOW'ST thou, O slave-cursed land!
  How, when the Chian's cup of guilt
    Was full to overflow, there came
    God's justice in the sword of flame
  That, red with slaughter to its hilt,
Blazed in the Cappadocian victor's hand?

    The heavens are still and far;
  But, not unheard of awful Jove,
    The sighing of the island slave
    Was answered, when the Ægean wave
  The keels of Mithridates clove,
And the vines shrivelled in the breath of war.

    "Robbers of Chios! hark,"
  The victor cried, "to Heaven's decree!
    Pluck your last cluster from the vine,
    Drain your last cup of Chian wine;
  Slaves of your slaves, your doom shall be,
In Colchian mines by Phasis rolling dark."

    Then rose the long lament
  From the hoar sea-god's dusky caves:
    The priestess rent her hair and cried,
    "Woe! woe! The gods are sleepless-eyed!"
  And, chained and scourged, the slaves of slaves,
The lords of Chios into exile went.

"The gods at last pay well,"
So Hellas sang her taunting song,
"The fisher in his net is caught,
The Chian hath his master bought";
And isle from isle, with laughter long,
Took up and sped the mocking parable.

Once more the slow, dumb years
Bring their avenging cycle round,
And, more than Hellas taught of old,
Our wiser lesson shall be told,
Of slaves uprising, freedom-crowned,
To break, not wield, the scourge wet with their blood and tears.

THE PROCLAMATION.

SAINT PATRICK, slave to Milcho of the herds
Of Ballymena, wakened with these words:
"Arise, and flee
Out from the land of bondage, and be free!"

Glad as a soul in pain, who hears from heaven
The angels singing of his sins forgiven,
And, wondering, sees
His prison opening to their golden keys,

He rose a man who laid him down a slave,
Shook from his locks the ashes of the grave,
And outward trod
Into the glorious liberty of God.

He cast the symbols of his shame away;
And, passing where the sleeping Milcho lay,
Though back and limb
Smarted with wrong, he prayed, "God pardon him!"

So went he forth: but in God's time he came
To light on Uilline's hills a holy flame;
And, dying, gave
The land a saint that lost him as a slave.

O dark, sad millions, patiently and dumb
Waiting for God, your hour, at last, has come,
And freedom's song
Breaks the long silence of your night of wrong!

Arise and flee! shake off the vile restraint
Of ages; but, like Ballymena's saint,
The oppressor spare,
Heap only on his head the coals of prayer.

Go forth, like him! like him return again,
To bless the land whereon in bitter pain
Ye toiled at first,
And heal with freedom what your slavery cursed.

AT PORT ROYAL.

THE tent-lights glimmer on the land,
  The ship-lights on the sea;
The night-wind smooths with drifting sand
  Our track on lone Tybee.

At last our grating keels outslide,
  Our good boats forward swing;
And while we ride the land-locked tide,
  Our negroes row and sing.

For dear the bondman holds his gifts
  Of music and of song:
The gold that kindly Nature sifts
  Among his sands of wrong;

The power to make his toiling days
  And poor home-comforts please;
The quaint relief of mirth that plays
  With sorrow's minor keys.

Another glow than sunset's fire
  Has filled the West with light,
Where field and garner, barn and byre
  Are blazing through the night.

The land is wild with fear and hate,
  The rout runs mad and fast;
From hand to hand, from gate to gate,
  The flaming brand is passed.

The lurid glow falls strong across
  Dark faces broad with smiles:
Not theirs the terror, hate, and loss
  That fire yon blazing piles.

With oar-strokes timing to their song,
  They weave in simple lays
The pathos of remembered wrong,
  The hope of better days, —

The triumph-note that Miriam sung,
  The joy of uncaged birds:
Softening with Afric's mellow tongue
  Their broken Saxon words.

SONG OF THE NEGRO BOATMEN.

O, praise an' tanks! De Lord he come
  To set de people free;
An' massa tink it day ob doom,
  An' we ob jubilee.

De Lord dat heap de Red-Sea waves
He jus' as 'trong as den;
He say de word: we las' night slaves;
To-day, de Lord's freemen.
De yam will grow, de cotton blow,
We 'll hab de rice an' corn;
O nebber you fear, if nebber you hear
De driver blow his horn!

Ole massa on he trabbels gone;
He leaf de land behind:
De Lord's breff blow him furder on,
Like corn-shuck in de wind.
We own de hoe, we own de plough,
We own de hands dat hold;
We sell de pig, we sell de cow,
But nebber chile be sold.
De yam will grow, de cotton blow,
We 'll hab de rice an' corn:
O nebber you fear, if nebber you hear
De driver blow his horn!

We pray de Lord: he gib us signs
Dat some day we be free;
De Norf-wind tell it to de pines,
De wild-duck to de sea;
We tink it when de church-bell ring,
We dream it in de dream;
De rice-bird mean it when he sing,
De eagle when he scream.
De yam will grow, de cotton blow,
We 'll hab de rice an' corn:
O nebber you fear, if nebber you hear
De driver blow his horn!

We know de promise nebber fail,
An' nebber lie de word;
So like de 'postles in de jail,
We waited for de Lord:

An' now he open ebery door,
  An' trow away de key;
He tink we lub him so before,
  We lub him better free.
    De yam will grow, de cotton blow,
      He 'll gib de rice an' corn:
    O nebber you fear, if nebber you hear
      De driver blow his horn!

So sing our dusky gondoliers;
  And, with a secret pain,
And smiles that seem akin to tears,
  We hear the wild refrain.

We dare not share the negro's trust,
  Nor yet his hope deny;
We only know that God is just,
  And every wrong shall die.

Rude seems the song; each swarthy face,
  Flame-lighted, ruder still:
We start to think that hapless race
  Must shape our good or ill;

That laws of changeless justice bind
  Oppressor with oppressed;
And, close as sin and suffering joined,
  We march to Fate abreast.

Sing on, poor hearts! your chant shall be
  Our sign of blight or bloom, —
The Vala-song of Liberty,
  Or death-rune of our doom!

ICHABOD!

SO fallen! so lost! the light withdrawn
Which once he wore!
The glory from his gray hairs gone
Forevermore!

Revile him not, — the Tempter hath
A snare for all;
And pitying tears, not scorn and wrath,
Befit his fall!

O, dumb be passion's stormy rage,
When he who might
Have lighted up and led his age
Falls back in night!

Scorn! would the angels laugh, to mark
A bright soul driven,
Fiend-goaded, down the endless dark,
From hope and heaven?

Let not the land, once proud of him,
Insult him now,
Nor brand with deeper shame his dim,
Dishonored brow.

But let its humbled sons, instead,
From sea to lake,
A long lament, as for the dead,
In sadness make.

Of all we loved and honored, naught
Save power remains, —
A fallen angel's pride of thought,
Still strong in chains.

All else is gone; from those great eyes
    The soul has fled:
When faith is lost, when honor dies,
    The man is dead!

Then, pay the reverence of old days
    To his dead fame;
Walk backward, with averted gaze,
    And hide the shame!

OUR STATE.

THE South-land boasts its teeming cane,
    The prairied West its heavy grain,
And sunset's radiant gates unfold
On rising marts and sands of gold!

Rough, bleak and hard, our little State
Is scant of soil, of limits strait;
Her yellow sands are sands alone,
Her only mines are ice and stone!

From Autumn frost to April rain,
Too long her winter woods complain;
From budding flower to falling leaf,
Her summer time is all too brief.

Yet, on her rocks, and on her sands,
And wintry hills, the school-house stands,
And what her rugged soil denies,
The harvest of the mind supplies.

The riches of the commonwealth
Are free, strong minds, and hearts of health;
And more to her than gold or grain,
The cunning hand and cultured brain.

For well she keeps her ancient stock,
The stubborn strength of Pilgrim Rock;
And still maintains, with milder laws,
And clearer light, the Good Old Cause!

Nor heeds the sceptic's puny hands,
While near her school the church-spire stands;
Nor fears the blinded bigot's rule,
While near her church-spire stands the school!

STANZAS FOR THE TIMES.

1850.

THE evil days have come, — the poor
Are made a prey;
Bar up the hospitable door,
Put out the fire-lights, point no more
The wanderer's way.

For Pity now is crime; the chain
Which binds our States
Is melted at her hearth in twain,
Is rusted by her tears' soft rain:
Close up her gates.

Our Union, like a glacier stirred
By voice below,
Or bell of kine, or wing of bird,
A beggar's crust, a kindly word
May overthrow!

Poor, whispering tremblers! — yet we boast
Our blood and name;
Bursting its century-bolted frost,
Each gray cairn on the Northman's coast
Cries out for shame!

O for the open firmament,
    The prairie free,
The desert hillside, cavern-rent,
The Pawnee's lodge, the Arab's tent,
    The Bushman's tree!

Than web of Persian loom most rare,
    Or soft divan,
Better the rough rock, bleak and bare,
Or hollow tree, which man may share
    With suffering man.

I hear a voice: "Thus saith the Law,
    Let Love be dumb;
Clasping her liberal hands in awe,
Let sweet-lipped Charity withdraw
    From hearth and home."

I hear another voice: "The poor
    Are thine to feed;
Turn not the outcast from thy door,
Nor give to bonds and wrong once more
    Whom God hath freed."

Dear Lord! between that law and thee
    No choice remains;
Yet not untrue to man's decree,
Though spurning its rewards, is he
    Who bears its pains.

Not mine Sedition's trumpet-blast
    And threatening word;
I read the lesson of the Past,
That firm endurance wins at last
    More than the sword.

O, clear-eyed Faith, and Patience, thou
    So calm and strong!
Lend strength to weakness, teach us how
The sleepless eyes of God look through
    This night of wrong!

A SABBATH SCENE.

SCARCE had the solemn Sabbath-bell
Ceased quivering in the steeple,
Scarce had the parson to his desk
Walked stately through his people,

When down the summer shaded street
  A wasted female figure,
With dusky brow and naked feet,
  Came rushing wild and eager.

She saw the white spire through the trees,
  She heard the sweet hymn swelling;
O, pitying Christ! a refuge give
  That poor one in thy dwelling!

Like a scared fawn before the hounds,
  Right up the aisle she glided,
While close behind her, whip in hand,
  A lank-haired hunter strided.

She raised a keen and bitter cry,
  To Heaven and Earth appealing; —
Were manhood's generous pulses dead?
  Had woman's heart no feeling?

A score of stout hands rose between
  The hunter and the flying;
Age clenched his staff, and maiden eyes
  Flashed tearful, yet defying.

"Who dares profane this house and day?"
  Cried out the angry pastor.
"Why, bless your soul, the wench 's a slave,
  And I 'm her lord and master!

"I 've law and gospel on my side,
  And who shall dare refuse me?"
Down came the parson, bowing low,
  "My good sir, pray excuse me!

"Of course I know your right divine
  To own and work and whip her;
Quick, deacon, throw that Polyglot
  Before the wench, and trip her!"

Plump dropped the holy tome, and o'er
  Its sacred pages stumbling,
Bound hand and foot, a slave once more,
  The hapless wretch lay trembling.

I saw the parson tie the knots,
  The while his flock addressing,
The Scriptural claims of slavery
  With text on text impressing.

"Although," said he, "on Sabbath day,
  All secular occupations
Are deadly sins, we must fulfil
  Our moral obligations:

"And this commends itself as one
  To every conscience tender;
As Paul sent back Onesimus,
  My Christian friends, we send her!"

Shriek rose on shriek, — the Sabbath air
  Her wild cries tore asunder;
I listened, with hushed breath, to hear
  God answering with his thunder!

All still! — the very altar's cloth
  Had smothered down her shrieking,
And, dumb, she turned from face to face,
  For human pity seeking!

I saw her dragged along the aisle,
  Her shackles harshly clanking;
I heard the parson, over all,
  The Lord devoutly thanking!

My brain took fire: "Is this," I cried,
  "The end of prayer and preaching?
Then down with pulpit, down with priest,
  And give us Nature's teaching!

"Foul shame and scorn be on ye all
  Who turn the good to evil,
And steal the Bible from the Lord,
  To give it to the Devil!

"Than garbled text or parchment law
  I own a statute higher;
And God is true, though every book
  And every man 's a liar!"

Just then I felt the deacon's hand
  In wrath my coat-tail seize on;
I heard the priest cry "Infidel!"
  The lawyer mutter "Treason!"

I started up, — where now were church,
  Slave, master, priest and people?
I only heard the supper-bell,
  Instead of clanging steeple.

But, on the open window's sill,
  O'er which the white blooms drifted,
The pages of a good old Book
  The wind of summer lifted.

And flower and vine, like angel wings
  Around the Holy Mother,
Waved softly there, as if God's truth
  And Mercy kissed each other.

And freely from the cherry-bough
  Above the casement swinging,
With golden bosom to the sun,
  The oriole was singing.

As bird and flower made plain of old
  The lesson of the Teacher,
So now I heard the written Word
  Interpreted by Nature!

For to my ear methought the breeze
  Bore Freedom's blessed word on;
THUS SAITH THE LORD: BREAK EVERY YOKE,
  UNDO THE HEAVY BURDEN!

RANTOUL.

ONE day, along the electric wire
  His manly word for Freedom sped;
We came next morn: that tongue of fire
  Said only, "He who spake is dead!"

Dead! while his voice was living yet,
  In echoes round the pillared dome!
Dead! while his blotted page lay wet
  With themes of state and loves of home!

Dead! in that crowning grace of time,
  That triumph of life's zenith hour!
Dead! while we watched his manhood's prime
  Break from the slow bud into flower!

Dead! he so great, and strong, and wise,
  While the mean thousands yet drew breath;
How deepened, through that dread surprise,
  The mystery and the awe of death!

From the high place whereon our votes
  Had borne him, clear, calm, earnest, fell
His first words, like the prelude notes
  Of some great anthem yet to swell.

We seemed to see our flag unfurled,
  Our champion waiting in his place
For the last battle of the world, —
  The Armageddon of the race.

Through him we hoped to speak the word
  Which wins the freedom of a land;
And lift, for human right, the sword
  Which dropped from Hampden's dying hand.

For he had sat at Sidney's feet,
  And walked with Pym and Vane apart;
And, through the centuries, felt the beat
  Of Freedom's march in Cromwell's heart.

He knew the paths the worthies held,
  Where England's best and wisest trod:
And, lingering, drank the springs that welled
  Beneath the touch of Milton's rod.

No wild enthusiast of the right,
  Self-poised and clear, he showed alway
The coolness of his northern night,
  The ripe repose of autumn's day.

His steps were slow, yet forward still
  He pressed where others paused or failed;
The calm star clomb with constant will, —
  The restless meteor flashed and paled!

Skilled in its subtlest wile, he knew
  And owned the higher ends of Law;
Still rose majestic on his view
  The awful Shape the schoolman saw.

Her home the heart of God; her voice
  The choral harmonies whereby
The stars, through all their spheres, rejoice,
  The rhythmic rule of earth and sky!

We saw his great powers misapplied
  To poor ambitions; yet, through all,
We saw him take the weaker side,
  And right the wronged, and free the thrall.

Now, looking o'er the frozen North
 For one like him in word and act,
To call her old, free spirit forth,
 And give her faith the life of fact, —

To break her party bonds of shame,
 And labor with the zeal of him
To make the Democratic name
 Of Liberty the synonyme, —

We sweep the land from hill to strand,
 We seek the strong, the wise, the brave,
And, sad of heart, return to stand
 In silence by a new-made grave!

There, where his breezy hills of home
 Look out upon his sail-white seas,
The sounds of winds and waters come,
 And shape themselves to words like these: —

"Why, murmuring, mourn that he, whose power
 Was lent to Party over-long,
Heard the still whisper at the hour
 He set his foot on Party wrong?

"The human life that closed so well
 No lapse of folly now can stain;
The lips whence Freedom's protest fell
 No meaner thought can now profane.

"Mightier than living voice his grave
 That lofty protest utters o'er;
Through roaring wind and smiting wave
 It speaks his hate of wrong once more.

"Men of the North! your weak regret
 Is wasted here; arise and pay
To freedom and to him your debt,
 By following where he led the way!"

BROWN OF OSSAWATOMIE.

JOHN BROWN OF OSSAWATOMIE spake on his dying day:
"I will not have to shrive my soul a priest in Slavery's pay.
But let some poor slave-mother whom I have striven to free,
With her children from the gallows-stair put up a prayer for me!"

John Brown of Ossawatomie, they led him out to die;
And lo! a poor slave-mother with her little child pressed nigh.
Then the bold, blue eye grew tender, and the old harsh face grew
mild,
As he stooped between the jeering ranks and kissed the negro's
child!

The shadows of his stormy life that moment fell apart;
And they who blamed the bloody hand forgave the loving heart.
That kiss from all its guilty means redeemed the good intent,
And round the grisly fighter's hair the martyr's aureole bent!

Perish with him the folly that seeks through evil good!
Long live the generous purpose unstained with human blood!
Not the raid of midnight terror, but the thought which underlies;
Not the borderer's pride of daring, but the Christian's sacrifice.

Never more may yon Blue Ridges the Northern rifle hear,
Nor see the light of blazing homes flash on the negro's spear.
But let the free-winged angel Truth their guarded passes scale,
To teach that right is more than might, and justice more than mail!

So vainly shall Virginia set her battle in array;
In vain her trampling squadrons knead the winter snow with clay.
She may strike the pouncing eagle, but she dares not harm the dove;
And every gate she bars to Hate shall open wide to Love!

THE RENDITION.

I HEARD the train's shrill whistle call,
I saw an earnest look beseech,
And rather by that look than speech
My neighbor told me all.

And, as I thought of Liberty
Marched handcuffed down that sworded street,
The solid earth beneath my feet
Reeled fluid as the sea.

I felt a sense of bitter loss, —
  Shame, tearless grief, and stifling wrath,
  And loathing fear, as if my path
A serpent stretched across.

All love of home, all pride of place,
  All generous confidence and trust,
  Sank smothering in that deep disgust
And anguish of disgrace.

Down on my native hills of June,
  And home's green quiet, hiding all,
  Fell sudden darkness, like the fall
Of midnight upon noon!

And Law, an unloosed maniac, strong,
  Blood-drunken, through the blackness trod,
  Hoarse-shouting in the ear of God
The blasphemy of wrong.

"O Mother, from thy memories proud,
  Thy old renown, dear Commonwealth,
  Lend this dead air a breeze of health,
And smite with stars this cloud.

"Mother of Freedom, wise and brave,
  Rise awful in thy strength," I said;
  Ah, me! I spake but to the dead;
I stood upon her grave!

6th mo., 1854.

LINES,

ON THE PASSAGE OF THE BILL TO PROTECT THE RIGHTS AND LIBERTIES OF THE PEOPLE OF THE STATE AGAINST THE FUGITIVE SLAVE ACT.

I SAID I stood upon thy grave,
  My Mother State, when last the moon
Of blossoms clomb the skies of June.

And, scattering ashes on my head,
I wore, undreaming of relief,
The sackcloth of thy shame and grief.

Again that moon of blossoms shines
On leaf and flower and folded wing,
And thou hast risen with the spring!

Once more thy strong maternal arms
Are round about thy children flung, —
A lioness that guards her young!

No threat is on thy closèd lips,
But in thine eye a power to smite
The mad wolf backward from its light.

Southward the baffled robber's track
Henceforth runs only; hereaway,
The fell lycanthrope finds no prey.

Henceforth, within thy sacred gates,
His first low howl shall downward draw
The thunder of thy righteous law.

Not mindless of thy trade and gain,
But, acting on the wiser plan,
Thou 'rt grown conservative of man.

So shalt thou clothe with life the hope,
Dream-painted on the sightless eyes
Of him who sang of Paradise, —

The vision of a Christian man,
In virtue as in stature great,
Embodied in a Christian State.

And thou, amidst thy sisterhood
Forbearing long, yet standing fast,
Shalt win their grateful thanks at last;

When North and South shall strive no more,
And all their feuds and fears be lost
In Freedom's holy Pentecost.

6th mo., 1855.

THE POOR VOTER ON ELECTION DAY.

THE proudest now is but my peer,
  The highest not more high;
To-day, of all the weary year,
  A king of men am I.
To-day, alike are great and small,
  The nameless and the known;

My palace is the people's hall,
  The ballot-box my throne!

Who serves to-day upon the list
  Beside the served shall stand;
Alike the brown and wrinkled fist,
  The gloved and dainty hand!
The rich is level with the poor,
  The weak is strong to-day;
And sleekest broadcloth counts no more
  Than homespun frock of gray.

To-day let pomp and vain pretence
  My stubborn right abide;
I set a plain man's common sense
  Against the pedant's pride.
To-day shall simple manhood try
  The strength of gold and land;
The wide world has not wealth to buy
  The power in my right hand!

While there 's a grief to seek redress,
  Or balance to adjust,
Where weighs our living manhood less
  Than Mammon's vilest dust, —
While there 's a right to need my vote,
  A wrong to sweep away,
Up! clouted knee and ragged coat!
  A man 's a man to-day!

THE EVE OF ELECTION.

FROM gold to gray
  Our mild sweet day
Of Indian Summer fades too soon;
  But tenderly
  Above the sea
Hangs, white and calm, the Hunter's moon.

In its pale fire
The village spire
Shows like the zodiac's spectral lance;
The painted walls
Whereon it falls
Transfigured stand in marble trance!

O'er fallen leaves
The west wind grieves,
Yet comes a seed-time round again;
And morn shall see
The State sown free
With baleful tares or healthful grain.

Along the street
The shadows meet
Of Destiny, whose hands conceal
The moulds of fate
That shape the State,
And make or mar the common weal.

Around I see
The powers that be;
I stand by Empire's primal springs;
And princes meet
In every street,
And hear the tread of uncrowned kings!

Hark! through the crowd
The laugh runs loud,
Beneath the sad, rebuking moon.
God save the land
A careless hand
May shake or swerve ere morrow's noon!

No jest is this;
One cast amiss
May blast the hope of Freedom's year.
O, take me where
Are hearts of prayer,
And foreheads bowed in reverent fear!

Not lightly fall
Beyond recall
The written scrolls a breath can float;
The crowning fact,
The kingliest act
Of Freedom, is the freeman's vote!

For pearls that gem
A diadem
The diver in the deep sea dies;
The regal right
We boast to-night
Is ours through costlier sacrifice:

The blood of Vane,
His prison pain
Who traced the path the Pilgrim trod,
And hers whose faith
Drew strength from death,
And prayed her Russell up to God!

Our hearts grow cold,
We lightly hold
A right which brave men died to gain;
The stake, the cord,
The axe, the sword,
Grim nurses at its birth of pain.

The shadow rend,
And o'er us bend,
O martyrs, with your crowns and palms,—
Breathe through these throngs
Your battle songs,
Your scaffold prayers, and dungeon psalms!

Look from the sky,
Like God's great eye,
Thou solemn moon, with searching beam;
Till in the sight
Of thy pure light
Our mean self-seekings meaner seem.

Shame from our hearts
Unworthy arts,
The fraud designed, the purpose dark;
And smite away
The hands we lay
Profanely on the sacred ark.

To party claims,
And private aims,
Reveal that august face of Truth,
Whereto are given
The age of heaven,
The beauty of immortal youth.

So shall our voice
Of sovereign choice
Swell the deep bass of duty done,
And strike the key
Of time to be,
When God and man shall speak as one!

LE MARAIS DU CYGNE.

A BLUSH as of roses
Where rose never grew!
Great drops on the bunch-grass,
But not of the dew!
A taint in the sweet air
For wild bees to shun!
A stain that shall never
Bleach out in the sun!

Back, steed of the prairies!
Sweet song-bird, fly back!
Wheel hither, bald vulture!
Gray wolf, call thy pack!

The foul human vultures
  Have feasted and fled;
The wolves of the Border
  Have crept from the dead.

From the hearths of their cabins,
  The fields of their corn,
Unwarned and unweaponed,
  The victims were torn, —
By the whirlwind of murder
  Swooped up and swept on
To the low, reedy fen-lands,
  The Marsh of the Swan.

With a vain plea for mercy
  No stout knee was crooked;
In the mouths of the rifles
  Right manly they looked.
How paled the May sunshine,
  O Marais du Cygne!
On death for the strong life,
  On red grass for green!

In the homes of their rearing,
  Yet warm with their lives,
Ye wait the dead only,
  Poor children and wives!
Put out the red forge-fire,
  The smith shall not come;
Unyoke the brown oxen,
  The ploughman lies dumb.

Wind slow from the Swan's Marsh,
  O dreary death train,
With pressed lips as bloodless
  As lips of the slain!
Kiss down the young eyelids,
  Smooth down the gray hairs;
Let tears quench the curses
  That burn through your prayers.

Strong man of the prairies,
  Mourn bitter and wild!
Wail, desolate woman!
  Weep, fatherless child!
But the grain of God springs up
  From ashes beneath,
And the crown of his harvest
  Is life out of death.

Not in vain on the dial
  The shade moves along,
To point the great contrasts
  Of right and of wrong:
Free homes and free altars,
  Free prairie and flood, —
The reeds of the Swan's Marsh,
  Whose bloom is of blood!

On the lintels of Kansas
  That blood shall not dry;
Henceforth the Bad Angel
  Shall harmless go by;
Henceforth to the sunset,
  Unchecked on her way,
Shall Liberty follow
  The march of the day.

BARBARA FRIETCHIE.

UP from the meadows rich with corn,
Clear in the cool September morn,

The clustered spires of Frederick stand
Green-walled by the hills of Maryland.

Round about them orchards sweep,
Apple- and peach-tree fruited deep,

Fair as a garden of the Lord
To the eyes of the famished rebel horde,

On that pleasant morn of the early fall
When Lee marched over the mountain-wall, —

Over the mountains winding down,
Horse and foot, into Frederick town.

Forty flags with their silver stars,
Forty flags with their crimson bars,

Flapped in the morning wind: the sun
Of noon looked down, and saw not one.

Up rose old Barbara Frietchie then,
Bowed with her fourscore years and ten;

Bravest of all in Frederick town,
She took up the flag the men hauled down;

In her attic-window the staff she set,
To show that one heart was loyal yet.

Up the street came the rebel tread,
Stonewall Jackson riding ahead.

Under his slouched hat left and right
He glanced; the old flag met his sight.

"Halt!"—the dust-brown ranks stood fast.
"Fire!"—out blazed the rifle-blast.

It shivered the window, pane and sash;
It rent the banner with seam and gash.

Quick, as it fell, from the broken staff
Dame Barbara snatched the silken scarf;

She leaned far out on the window-sill,
And shook it forth with a royal will.

"Shoot, if you must, this old gray head,
But spare your country's flag," she said.

A shade of sadness, a blush of shame,
Over the face of the leader came;

The nobler nature within him stirred
To life at that woman's deed and word:

"Who touches a hair of yon gray head
Dies like a dog! March on!" he said.

All day long through Frederick street
Sounded the tread of marching feet:

All day long that free flag tost.
Over the heads of the rebel host.

Ever its torn folds rose and fell
On the loyal winds that loved it well;

And through the hill-gaps sunset light
Shone over it with a warm good-night.

Barbara Frietchie's work is o'er,
And the Rebel rides on his raids no more.

Honor to her! and let a tear
Fall, for her sake, on Stonewall's bier.

Over Barbara Frietchie's grave,
Flag of Freedom and Union, wave!

Peace and order and beauty draw
Round thy symbol of light and law;

And ever the stars above look down
On thy stars below in Frederick town!

LAUS DEO.

ON HEARING THE BELLS RING FOR THE CONSTITUTIONAL AMENDMENT ABOLISHING SLAVERY IN THE UNITED STATES.

IT is done!
Clang of bell and roar of gun
Send the tidings up and down.
How the belfries rock and reel,
How the great guns, peal on peal,
Fling the joy from town to town!

Ring, O bells!
Every stroke exulting tells
Of the burial hour of crime.
Loud and long, that all may hear,
Ring for every listening ear
Of Eternity and Time!

Let us kneel:
God's own voice is in that peal,
And this spot is holy ground.
Lord, forgive us! What are we,
That our eyes this glory see,
That our ears have heard the sound!

For the Lord
On the whirlwind is abroad;
In the earthquake he has spoken;
He has smitten with his thunder
The iron walls asunder,
And the gates of brass are broken!

Loud and long
Lift the old exulting song,
Sing with Miriam by the sea:
He has cast the mighty down;
Horse and rider sink and drown;
He has triumphed gloriously!

Did we dare,
In our agony of prayer,
Ask for more than he has done?
When was ever his right hand
Over any time or land
Stretched as now beneath the sun!

How they pale,
Ancient myth, and song, and tale,
In this wonder of our days,
When the cruel rod of war
Blossoms white with righteous law,
And the wrath of man is praise.

Blotted out!
All within and all about
Shall a fresher life begin;
Freer breathe the universe
As it rolls its heavy curse
On the dead and buried sin.

It is done!
In the circuit of the sun
Shall the sound thereof go forth.
It shall bid the sad rejoice,
It shall give the dumb a voice,
It shall belt with joy the earth!

Ring and swing
Bells of joy! on morning's wing
Send the song of praise abroad;
With a sound of broken chains,
Tell the nations that He reigns,
Who alone is Lord and God!

Cambridge: Electrotyped and Printed by Welch, Bigelow, & Co.

Voices of Nature.

BY

WILLIAM CULLEN BRYANT.

With Illustrations.

NEW YORK:
D. APPLETON AND COMPANY,
90, 92 & 94 GRAND ST.
BOSTON: FIELDS, OSGOOD & CO.
1869.

[These selections from the Poems of Mr. Bryant are made by the publishers to supply a popular demand for the rural poems in a single inexpensive volume.]

CONTENTS.

VOICES OF NATURE.

JUNE.

I GAZED upon the glorious sky
  And the green mountains round,
And thought that when I came to lie
  At rest within the ground,
'Twere pleasant that in flowery June,
When brooks send up a cheerful tune,
  And groves a joyous sound,
The sexton's hand, my grave to make,
The rich, green mountain turf should break.

A cell within the frozen mould,
  A coffin borne through sleet,
And icy clods above it rolled,
  While fierce the tempests beat—
Away !—I will not think of these—
Blue be the sky and soft the breeze,
  Earth green beneath the feet,
And be the damp mould gently pressed
Into my narrow place of rest.

There, through the long, long summer hours,
  The golden light should lie,
And thick young herbs and groups of flowers
  Stand in their beauty by.
The oriole should build and tell
His love-tale close beside my cell;
  The idle butterfly
Should rest him there, and there be heard
The housewife bee and humming-bird.

And what if cheerful shouts at noon
  Come, from the village sent,
Or songs of maids, beneath the moon,
  With fairy laughter blent?
And what if, in the evening light,
Betrothed lovers walk in sight
  Of my low monument?
I would the lovely scene around
Might know no sadder sight nor sound.

I know, I know I should not see
  The season's glorious show,
Nor would its brightness shine for me,
  Nor its wild music flow;
But if, around my place of sleep,
The friends I love should come to weep,
  They might not haste to go.
Soft airs, and song, and light, and bloom,
Should keep them lingering by my tomb.

These to their softened hearts should bear
  The thought of what has been,
And speak of one who cannot share
  The gladness of the scene;
Whose part, in all the pomp that fills
The circuit of the summer hills,
  Is—that his grave is green;
And deeply would their hearts rejoice
To hear again his living voice.

THANATOPSIS.

TO him who in the love of Nature holds
Communion with her visible forms, she speaks
A various language; for his gayer hours
She has a voice of gladness, and a smile
And eloquence of beauty, and she glides
Into his darker musings, with a mild
And healing sympathy, that steals away
Their sharpness, ere he is aware. When thoughts
Of the last bitter hour come like a blight
Over thy spirit, and sad images
Of the stern agony, and shroud, and pall,
And breathless darkness, and the narrow house,
Make thee to shudder, and grow sick at heart;—
Go forth, under the open sky, and list
To Nature's teachings, while from all around—
Earth and her waters, and the depths of air—
Comes a still voice—Yet a few days, and thee
The all-beholding sun shall see no more
In all his course; nor yet in the cold ground,
Where thy pale form was laid, with many tears,
Nor in the embrace of ocean, shall exist
Thy image. Earth, that nourished thee, shall claim
Thy growth, to be resolved to earth again,
And, lost each human trace, surrendering up
Thine individual being, shalt thou go
To mix for ever with the elements,
To be a brother to the insensible rock
And to the sluggish clod, which the rude swain
Turns with his share, and treads upon. The oak
Shall send his roots abroad, and pierce thy mould.

Yet not to thine eternal resting place
Shalt thou retire alone, nor couldst thou wish
Couch more magnificent. Thou shalt lie down
With patriarchs of the infant world—with kings,
The powerful of the earth—the wise, the good,
Fair forms, and hoary seers of ages past,
All in one mighty sepulchre. The hills
Rock-ribbed and ancient as the sun; the vales
Stretching in pensive quietness between;
The venerable woods; rivers that move
In majesty, and the complaining brooks
That make the meadows green; and, poured round all,
Old ocean's gray and melancholy waste,—
Are but the solemn decorations all
Of the great tomb of man. The golden sun,
The planets, all the infinite host of heaven,
Are shining on the sad abodes of death,
Through the still lapse of ages. All that tread
The globe are but a handful to the tribes
That slumber in its bosom.—Take the wings
Of morning, traverse Barca's desert sands,
Or lose thyself in the continuous woods
Where rolls the Oregan, and hears no sound,
Save his own dashings—yet—the dead are there:
And millions in those solitudes, since first
The flight of years began, have laid them down
In their last sleep—the dead reign there alone.
So shalt thou rest, and what if thou withdraw
In silence from the living, and no friend
Take note of thy departure? All that breathe
Will share thy destiny. The gay will laugh
When thou art gone, the solemn brood of care
Plod on, and each one as before will chase

His favourite phantom; yet all these shall leave
Their mirth and their employments, and shall come,
And make their bed with thee. As the long train
Of ages glide away, the sons of men,—
The youth in life's green spring, and he who goes
In the full strength of years, matron, and maid,
And the sweet babe, and the gray-headed man.—
Shall one by one be gathered to thy side,
By those who in their turn shall follow them.

So live, that when thy summons comes to join
The innumerable caravan, which moves
To that mysterious realm, where each shall take
His chamber in the silent halls of death,
Thou go not like the quarry-slave at night,
Scourged to his dungeon, but, sustained and soothed
By an unfaltering trust, approach thy grave
Like one who wraps the drapery of his couch
About him, and lies down to pleasant dreams.

THE YELLOW VIOLET.

WHEN beechen buds begin to swell,
And woods the blue-bird's warble know,
The yellow violet's modest bell
Peeps from the last year's leaves below

Ere russet fields their green resume,
Sweet flower, I love, in forest bare,
To meet thee, when thy faint perfume
Alone is in the virgin air.

Of all her train, the hands of Spring
  First plant thee in the watery mould,
And I have seen thee blossoming
  Beside the snow-bank's edges cold.

Thy parent sun, who bade thee view
  Pale skies, and chilling moisture sip,
Has bathed thee in his own bright hue,
  And streaked with jet thy glowing lip.

Yet slight thy form, and low thy seat,
  And earthward bent thy gentle eye,
Unapt the passing view to meet,
  When loftier flowers are flaunting nigh.

Oft, in the sunless April day,
  Thy early smile has stayed my walk;
But midst the gorgeous blooms of May,
  I passed thee on thy humble stalk.

So they, who climb to wealth, forget
  The friends in darker fortunes tried.
I copied them—but I regret
  That I should ape the ways of pride.

And when again the genial hour
  Awakes the painted tribes of light,
I'll not o'erlook the modest flower
  That made the woods of April bright.

INSCRIPTION FOR THE ENTRANCE TO A WOOD.

STRANGER, if thou hast learned a truth which needs
No school of long experience, that the world
Is full of guilt and misery, and hast seen
Enough of all its sorrows, crimes, and cares,
To tire thee of it, enter this wild wood
And view the haunts of Nature. The calm shade
Shall bring a kindred calm, and the sweet breeze
That makes the green leaves dance, shall waft a balm
To thy sick heart. Thou wilt find nothing here
Of all that pained thee in the haunts of men,
And made thee loathe thy life. The primal curse
Fell, it is true, upon the unsinning earth,
But not in vengeance. God hath yoked to guilt
Her pale tormentor, misery. Hence, these shades
Are still the abodes of gladness; the thick roof
Of green and stirring branches is alive
And musical with birds, that sing and sport
In wantonness of spirit; while below
The squirrel, with raised paws and form erect,
Chirps merrily. Throngs of insects in the shade
Try their thin wings and dance in the warm beam
That waked them into life. Even the green trees
Partake the deep contentment; as they bend
To the soft winds, the sun from the blue sky
Looks in and sheds a blessing on the scene.
Scarce less the cleft-born wild-flower seems to enjoy
Existence, than the winged plunderer

That sucks its sweets. The mossy rocks themselves,
And the old and ponderous trunks of prostrate trees
That lead from knoll to knoll a causey rude,
Or bridge the sunken brook, and their dark roots,
With all their earth upon them, twisting high,
Breathe fixed tranquillity. The rivulet
Sends forth glad sounds, and tripping o'er its bed
Of pebbly sands, or leaping down the rocks,
Seems, with continuous laughter, to rejoice
In its own being. Softly tread the marge,
Lest from her midway perch thou scare the wren
That dips her bill in water. The cool wind,
That stirs the stream in play, shall come to thee,
Like one that loves thee nor will let thee pass
Ungreeted, and shall give its light embrace.

TO A WATERFOWL.

WHITHER, midst falling dew,
While glow the heavens with the last steps of day,
Far, through their rosy depths, dost thou pursue
Thy solitary way?

Vainly the fowler's eye
Might mark thy distant flight to do thee wrong,
As, darkly seen against the crimson sky,
Thy figure floats along.

Seek'st thou the plashy brink
Of weedy lake, or marge of river wide,
Or where the rocking billows rise and sink
On the chafed ocean side?

There is a Power whose care
Teaches thy way along that pathless coast,—
The desert and illimitable air,—
Lone wandering, but not lost.

All day thy wings have fanned,
At that far height, the cold, thin atmosphere,
Yet stoop not, weary, to the welcome land,
Though the dark night is near.

And soon that toil shall end;
Soon shalt thou find a summer home and rest,
And scream among thy fellows; reeds shall bend,
Soon, o'er thy sheltered nest.

Thou'rt gone, the abyss of heaven
Hath swallowed up thy form; yet, on my heart
Deeply hath sunk the lesson thou hast given,
And shall not soon depart.

He who, from zone to zone,
Guides through the boundless sky thy certain flight,
In the long way that I must tread alone,
Will lead my steps aright.

GREEN RIVER.

WHEN breezes are soft and skies are fair,
I steal an hour from study and care,
And hie me away to the woodland scene,
Where wanders the stream with waters of green,
As if the bright fringe of herbs on its brink
Had given their stain to the wave they drink;
And they, whose meadows it murmurs through,
Have named the stream from its own fair hue.

Yet pure its waters—its shallows are bright
With coloured pebbles and sparkles of light,
And clear the depths where its eddies play,
And dimples deepen and whirl away,
And the plane-tree's speckled arms o'ershoot
The swifter current that mines its root,
Through whose shifting leaves, as you walk the hill,
The quivering glimmer of sun and rill
With a sudden flash on the eye is thrown,
Like the ray that streams from the diamond-stone.
Oh, loveliest there the spring days come,
With blossoms, and birds, and wild bees' hum,
The flowers of summer are fairest there,
And freshest the breath of the summer air;
And sweetest the golden autumn day
In silence and sunshine glides away.

Yet, fair as thou art, thou shunnest to glide,
Beautiful stream! by the village side;
But windest away from haunts of men,
To quiet valley and shaded glen;
And forest, and meadow, and slope of hill,
Around thee, are lonely, lovely, and still.
Lonely—save when, by thy rippling tides,
From thicket to thicket the angler glides;
Or the simpler comes, with basket and book,
For herbs of power on thy banks to look,
Or haply, some idle dreamer, like me,
To wander, and muse, and gaze on thee.
Still—save the chirp of birds that feed
On the river cherry and seedy reed,
And thy own wild music gushing out
With mellow murmur or fairy shout,

From dawn to the blush of another day,
Like traveller singing along his way.

That fairy music I never hear,
Nor gaze on those waters so green and clear,
And mark them winding away from sight,
Darkened with shade or flashing with light,
While o'er them the vine to its thicket clings,
And the zephyr stoops to freshen his wings,
But I wish that fate had left me free
To wander these quiet haunts with thee,
Till the eating cares of earth should depart,
And the peace of the scene pass into my heart;
And I envy thy stream, as it glides along,
Through its beautiful banks, in a trance of song.

Though forced to drudge for the dregs of men,
And scrawl strange words with the barbarous pen,
And mingle among the jostling crowd,
Where the sons of strife are subtle and loud—
I often come to this quiet place,
To breathe the airs that ruffle thy face,
And gaze upon thee in silent dream,
For in thy lonely and lovely stream
An image of that calm life appears
That won my heart in my greener years.

A WINTER PIECE.

THE time has been that these wild solitudes,
Yet beautiful as wild, were trod by me
Oftener than now; and when the ills of life
Had chafed my spirit—when the unsteady pulse

Beat with strange flutterings—I would wander forth
And seek the woods. The sunshine on my path
Was to me as a friend. The swelling hills,
The quiet dells retiring far between,
With gentle invitation to explore
Their windings, were a calm society
That talked with me and soothed me. Then the chant
Of birds, and chime of brooks, and soft caress
Of the fresh sylvan air, made me forget
The thoughts that broke my peace, and I began
To gather simples by the fountain's brink,
And lose myself in day dreams. While I stood
In nature's loneliness, I was with one
With whom I early grew familiar, one
Who never had a frown for me, whose voice
Never rebuked me for the hours I stole
From cares I loved not, but of which the world
Deems highest, to converse with her. When shrieked
The bleak November winds, and smote the woods,
And the brown fields were herbless, and the shades,
That met above the merry rivulet,
Were spoiled, I sought, I loved them still; they seemed
Like old companions in adversity.
Still there was beauty in my walks; the brook,
Bordered with sparkling frost-work, was as gay
As with its fringe of summer flowers. Afar,
The village with its spires, the path of streams,
And dim receding valleys, hid before
By interposing trees, lay visible
Through the bare grove, and my familiar haunts
Seemed new to me. Nor was I slow to come
Among them, when the clouds, from their still skirts,
Had shaken down on earth the feathery snow,

And all was white. The pure keen air abroad,
Albeit it breathed no scent of herb, nor heard
Love-call of bird nor merry hum of bee,
Was not the air of death. Bright mosses crept
Over the spotted trunks, and the close buds,
That lay along the boughs, instinct with life,
Patient, and waiting the soft breath of Spring,
Feared not the piercing spirit of the North.
The snow-bird twittered on the beechen bough,
And 'neath the hemlock, whose thick branches bent
Beneath its bright cold burden, and kept dry
A circle, on the earth, of withered leaves,
The partridge found a shelter. Through the snow
The rabbit sprang away. The lighter track
Of fox, and the raccoon's broad path, were there,
Crossing each other. From his hollow tree,
The squirrel was abroad, gathering the nuts
Just fallen, that asked the winter cold and sway
Of winter blast to shake them from their hold.

But Winter has yet brighter scenes,—he boasts
Splendors beyond what gorgeous Summer knows;
Or Autumn with his many fruits, and woods
All flushed with many hues. Come when the rains
Have glazed the snow, and clothed the trees with ice,
While the slant sun of February pours
Into the bowers a flood of light. Approach!
The incrusted surface shall upbear thy steps,
And the broad arching portals of the grove
Welcome thy entering. Look! the massy trunks
Are cased in the pure crystal; each light spray,
Nodding and tinkling in the breath of heaven,
Is studded with its trembling water-drops,

That glimmer with an amethystine light.
But round the parent stem the long low boughs
Bend, in a glittering ring, and arbors hide
The glassy floor. Oh! you might deem the spot
The spacious cavern of some virgin mine,
Deep in the womb of earth—where the gems grow,
And diamonds put forth radiant rods and bud
With amethyst and topaz—and the place
Lit up, most royally, with the pure beam
That dwells in them. Or haply the vast hall
Of fairy palace, that outlasts the night,
And fades not in the glory of the sun;—
Where crystal columns send forth slender shafts
And crossing arches; and fantastic aisles
Wind from the sight in brightness, and are lost
Among the crowded pillars. Raise thine eye;
Thou seest no cavern roof, no palace vault;
There the blue sky and the white drifting cloud
Look in. Again the wildered fancy dreams
Of spouting fountains, frozen as they rose,
And fixed, with all their branching jets, in air,
And all their sluices sealed. All, all is light;
Light without shade. But all shall pass away
With the next sun. From numberless vast trunks,
Loosened, the crashing ice shall make a sound
Like the far roar of rivers, and the eve
Shall close o'er the brown woods as it was wont.

And it is pleasant, when the noisy streams
Are just set free, and milder suns melt off
The plashy snow, save only the firm drift
In the deep glen or the close shade of pines,—
'Tis pleasant to behold the wreaths of smoke

Roll up among the maples of the hill,
Where the shrill sound of youthful voices wakes
The shriller echo, as the clear pure lymph,
That from the wounded trees, in twinkling drops,
Falls, mid the golden brightness of the morn,
Is gathered in with brimming pails, and oft,
Wielded by sturdy hands, the stroke of axe
Makes the woods ring. Along the quiet air,
Come and float calmly off the soft light clouds,
Such as you see in summer, and the winds
Scarce stir the branches. Lodged in sunny cleft,
Where the cold breezes come not, blooms alone
The little wind-flower, whose just opened eye
Is blue as the spring heaven it gazes at—
Startling the loiterer in the naked groves
With unexpected beauty, for the time
Of blossoms and green leaves is yet afar.
And ere it comes, the encountering winds shall oft
Muster their wrath again, and rapid clouds
Shade heaven, and bounding on the frozen earth
Shall fall their volleyed stores, rounded like hail
And white like snow, and the loud North again
Shall buffet the vexed forest in his rage.

ODE FOR AN AGRICULTURAL CELEBRATION.

FAR back in the ages,
The plough with wreaths was crowned;
The hands of kings and sages
Entwined the chaplet round;

Till men of spoil disdained the toil
  By which the world was nourished,
And dews of blood enriched the soil
  Where green their laurels flourished.
—Now the world her fault repairs—
  The guilt that stains her story,
And weeps her crimes amid the cares
  That formed her earliest glory.

The proud throne shall crumble,
  The diadem shall wane,
The tribes of earth shall humble
  The pride of those who reign;
And War shall lay his pomp away;—
  The famė that heroes cherish,
The glory earned in deadly fray,
  Shall fade, decay, and perish.
Honor waits, o'er all the Earth,
  Through endless generations,
The art that calls her harvests forth,
  And feeds the expectant nations.

THE RIVULET.

THIS little rill, that from the springs
  Of yonder grove its current brings,
Plays on the slope awhile, and then
Goes prattling into groves again,
Oft to its warbling waters drew
My little feet, when life was new.

When woods in early green were dressed,
And from the chambers of the west
The warmer breezes, travelling out,
Breathed the new scent of flowers about,
My truant steps from home would stray,
Upon its grassy side to play,
List the brown thrasher's vernal hymn,
And crop the violet on its brim,
With blooming cheek and open brow,
As young and gay, sweet rill, as thou.

And when the days of boyhood came,
And I had grown in love with fame,
Duly I sought thy banks, and tried
My first rude numbers by thy side.
Words cannot tell how bright and gay
The scenes of life before me lay.
Then glorious hopes, that now to speak
Would bring the blood into my cheek,
Passed o'er me ; and I wrote, on high,
A name I deemed should never die.

Years change thee not. Upon yon hill
The tall old maples, verdant still,
Yet tell, in grandeur of decay,
How swift the years have passed away,
Since first, a child, and half afraid,
I wandered in the forest shade.
Thou, ever joyous rivulet,
Dost dimple, leap, and prattle yet ;
And sporting with the sands that pave
The winding of thy silver wave,
And dancing to thy own wild chime,
Thou laughest at the lapse of time.
The same sweet sounds are in my ear
My early childhood loved to hear ;
As pure thy limpid waters run ;
As bright they sparkle to the sun ;
As fresh and thick the bending ranks
Of herbs that line thy oozy banks ;
The violet there, in soft May dew,
Comes up, as modest and as blue ;
As green amid thy current's stress,
Floats the scarce-rooted watercress :

And the brown ground-bird, in thy glen,
Still chirps as merrily as then.

Though changest not—but I am changed,
Since first thy pleasant banks I ranged;
And the grave stranger, come to see
The play-place of his infancy,
Has scarce a single trace of him
Who sported once upon thy brim.
The visions of my youth are past—
Too bright, too beautiful to last.
I've tried the world—it wears no more
The coloring of romance it wore.
Yet well has Nature kept the truth
She promised in my earliest youth.
The radiant beauty shed abroad
On all the glorious works of God,
Shows freshly, to my sobered eye,
Each charm it wore in days gone by.

A few brief years shall pass away,
And I, all trembling, weak, and gray,
Bowed to the earth, which waits to fold
My ashes in the embracing mould,
(If haply the dark will of fate
Indulge my life so long a date),
May come for the last time to look
Upon my childhood's favorite brook.
Then dimly on my eye shall gleam
The sparkle of thy dancing stream;
And faintly on my ear shall fall
Thy prattling current's merry call;
Yet shalt thou flow as glad and bright
As when thou met'st my infant sight.

And I shall sleep—and on thy side,
As ages after ages glide,
Children their early sports shall try,
And pass to hoary age and die.
But thou, unchanged from year to year,
Gayly shalt play and glitter here;
Amid young flowers and tender grass
Thy endless infancy shalt pass;
And, singing down thy narrow glen,
Shalt mock the fading race of men.

MARCH.

THE stormy March is come at last,
With wind, and cloud, and changing skies
I hear the rushing of the blast,
That through the snowy valley flies.

Ah, passing few are they who speak,
Wild stormy month! in praise of thee;
Yet, though thy winds are loud and bleak,
Thou art a welcome month to me.

For thou, to northern lands, again
The glad and glorious sun dost bring,
And thou hast joined the gentle train
And wear'st the gentle name of Spring.

And, in thy reign of blast and storm,
Smiles many a long, bright, sunny day,
When the changed winds are soft and warm,
And heaven puts on the blue of May.

Then sing aloud the gushing rills,
  In joy that they again are free,
And, brightly leaping down the hills,
  Begin their journey to the sea.

The year's departing beauty hides
  Of wintry storms the sullen threat;
But in thy sternest frown abides
  A look of kindly promise yet.

Thou bring'st the hope of those calm skies,
  And that soft time of sunny showers,
When the wide bloom, on earth that lies,
  Seems of a brighter world than ours.

SUMMER WIND.

IT is a sultry day; the sun has drunk
  The dew that lay upon the morning grass;
There is no rustling in the lofty elm
That canopies my dwelling, and its shade
Scarce cools me. All is silent, save the faint
And interrupted murmur of the bee,
Settling on the sick flowers, and then again
Instantly on the wing. The plants around
Feel the too potent fervors; the tall maize
Rolls up its long green leaves; the clover droops
Its tender foliage, and declines its blooms.
But far, in the fierce sunshine, tower the hills,
With all their growth of woods, silent and stern,
As if the scorching heat and dazzling light
Were but an element they loved. Bright clouds,

Motionless pillars of the brazen heaven,—
Their bases on the mountains—their white tops
Shining in the far ether,—fire the air
With a reflected radiance, and make turn
The gazer's eye away. For me, I lie
Languidly in the shade, where the thick turf,
Yet virgin from the kisses of the sun,
Retains some freshness, and I woo the wind
That still delays his coming. Why so slow,
Gentle and voluble spirit of the air?
Oh, come and breathe upon the fainting earth
Coolness and life. Is it that in his caves
He hears me? See, on yonder woody ridge,
The pine is bending his proud top, and now
Among the nearer groves, chestnut and oak
Are tossing their green boughs about. He comes!
Lo, where the grassy meadow runs in waves!
The deep distressful silence of the scene
Breaks up with mingling of unnumbered sounds
And universal motion. He is come,
Shaking a shower of blossoms from the shrubs,
And bearing on their fragrance; and he brings
Music of birds, and rustling of young boughs,
And sound of swaying branches, and the voice
Of distant waterfalls. All the green herbs
Are stirring in his breath; a thousand flowers,
By the roadside and the borders of the brook,
Nod gayly to each other; glossy leaves
Are twinkling in the sun, as if the dew
Were on them yet, and silver waters break
Into small waves and sparkle as he comes.

MONUMENT MOUNTAIN.

THOU who wouldst see the lovely and the wild
 Mingled in harmony on Nature's face,
Ascend our rocky mountains. Let thy foot
Fail not with weariness, for on their tops
The beauty and the majesty of earth,
Spread wide beneath, shall make thee to forget
The steep and toilsome way. There, as thou stand'st,
The haunts of men below thee, and around
The mountain summits, thy expanding heart
Shall feel a kindred with that loftier world
To which thou art translated, and partake
The enlargement of thy vision. Thou shalt look
Upon the green and rolling forest tops,
And down into the secrets of the glens,
And streams, that with their bordering thickets strive
To hide their windings. Thou shalt gaze, at once,
Here on white villages, and tilth, and herds,
And swarming roads, and there on solitudes
That only hear the torrent, and the wind,
And eagle's shriek. There is a precipice
That seems a fragment of some mighty wall,
Built by the hand that fashioned the old world,
To separate its nations, and thrown down
When the flood drowned them. To the north, a path
Conducts you up the narrow battlement.
Steep is the western side, shaggy and wild
With mossy trees, and pinnacles of flint,
And many a hanging crag. But, to the east,
Sheer to the vale go down the bare old cliffs,—
Huge pillars, that in middle heaven upbear

Their weather-beaten capitals, here dark
With moss, the growth of centuries, and there
Of chalky whiteness where the thunderbolt
Has splintered them. It is a fearful thing
To stand upon the beetling verge, and see
Where storm and lightning, from that huge gray wall,
Have tumbled down vast blocks, and at the base
Dashed them in fragments, and to lay thine ear
Over the dizzy depth, and hear the sound
Of winds, that struggle with the woods below,
Come up like ocean murmurs. But the scene
Is lovely round; a beautiful river there
Wanders amid the fresh and fertile meads,
The paradise he made unto himself,
Mining the soil for ages. On each side
The fields swell upward to the hills; beyond,
Above the hills, in the blue distance, rise
The mountain columns with which earth props heaven.

There is a tale about these reverend rocks,
A sad tradition of unhappy love,
And sorrows borne and ended, long ago,
When over these fair vales the savage sought
His game in the thick woods. There was a maid,
The fairest of the Indian maids, bright-eyed,
With wealth of raven tresses, a light form,
And a gay heart. About her cabin door
The wide old woods resounded with her song
And fairy laughter all the summer day.
She loved her cousin; such a love was deemed,
By the morality of those stern tribes,
Incestuous, and she struggled hard and long
Against her love, and reasoned with her heart,

As simple Indian maiden might. In vain.
Then her eye lost its lustre, and her step
Its lightness, and the gray-haired men that passed
Her dwelling, wondered that they heard no more
The accustomed song and laugh of her, whose looks
Were like the cheerful smile of Spring, they said,
Upon the winter of their age. She went
To weep where no eye saw, and was not found
When all the merry girls were met to dance,
And all the hunters of the tribe were out;
Nor when they gathered from the rustling husk
The shining ear; nor when, by the river's side,
They pulled the grape and startled the wild shades
With sounds of mirth. The keen-eyed Indian dames
Would whisper to each other, as they saw
Her wasting form, and say *the girl will die!*

One day into the bosom of a friend,
A playmate of her young and innocent years,
She poured her griefs. "Thou know'st, and thou alone,"
She said, "for I have told thee all, my love
And guilt and sorrow. I am sick of life.
All night I weep in darkness, and the morn
Glares on me, as upon a thing accursed,
That has no business on the earth. I hate
The pastimes and the pleasant toils that once
I loved; the cheerful voices of my friends
Sound in my ear like mockings, and, at night,
In dreams, my mother, from the land of souls,
Calls me and chides me. All that look on me
Do seem to know my shame; I cannot bear
Their eyes; I cannot from my heart root out
The love that wrings it so, and I must die."

It was a summer morning, and they went
To this old precipice. About the cliffs
Lay garlands, ears of maize, and shaggy skins
Of wolf and bear, the offerings of the tribe
Here made to the Great Spirit; for they deemed,
Like worshippers of the elder time, that God
Doth walk on the high places and affect
The earth-o'erlooking mountains. She had on
The ornaments with which her father loved
To deck the beauty of his bright-eyed girl,
And bade her wear when stranger warriors came
To be his guests. Here the friends sat them down,
And sang, all day, old songs of love and death,
And decked the poor wan victim's hair with flowers,
And prayed that safe and swift might be her way
To that calm world of sunshine, where no grief
Makes the heart heavy and the eyelids red.
Beautiful lay the region of her tribe
Below her—waters resting in the embrace
Of the wide forest, and maize-planted glades
Opening amid the leafy wilderness.
She gazed upon it long, and at the sight
Of her own village peeping through the trees,
And her own dwelling, and the cabin roof
Of him she loved with an unlawful love,
And came to die for, a warm gush of tears
Ran from her eyes. But when the sun grew low
And the hill shadows long, she threw herself
From the steep rock and perished. There was scooped
Upon the mountain's southern slope, a grave;
And there they laid her, in the very garb
With which the maiden decked herself for death,
With the same withering wild flowers in her hair.

And o'er the mould that covered her, the tribe
Built up a simple monument, a cone
Of small loose stones. Thenceforward all who passed,
Hunter, and dame, and virgin, laid a stone
In silence on the pile. It stands there yet.
And Indians from the distant West, who come
To visit where their fathers' bones are laid,
Yet tell the sorrowful tale, and to this day
The mountain where the hapless maiden died
Is called the Mountain of the Monument.

AFTER A TEMPEST.

THE day had been a day of wind and storm;
The wind was laid, the storm was overpast,
And stooping from the zenith, bright and warm,
Shone the great sun on the wide earth at last.
I stood upon the upland slope, and cast
My eye upon a broad and beauteous scene,
Where the vast plain lay girt by mountains vast,
And hills o'er hills lifted their heads of green,
With pleasant vales scooped out and villages between.

The rain-drops glistened on the trees around,
Whose shadows on the tall grass were not stirred,
Save when a shower of diamonds, to the ground,
Was shaken by the flight of startled bird;
For birds were warbling round, and bees were heard
About the flowers; the cheerful rivulet sung
And gossipped, as he hastened ocean-ward;
To the gray oak the squirrel, chiding, clung,
And chirping from the ground the grasshopper upsprung.

And from beneath the leaves that kept them dry
Flew many a glittering insect here and there,
And darted up and down the butterfly,
That seemed a living blossom of the air.
The flocks came scattering from the thicket, where
The violent rain had pent them; in the way
Strolled groups of damsels frolicsome and fair;
The farmer swung the scythe or turned the hay,
And 'twixt the heavy swaths his children were at play.

It was a scene of peace—and, like a spell,
Did that serene and golden sunlight fall
Upon the motionless wood that clothed the fell,
And precipice upspringing like a wall,
And glassy river and white waterfall,
And happy living things that trod the bright
And beauteous scene; while far beyond them all,
On many a lovely valley, out of sight,
Was poured from the blue heavens the same soft golden
light.

I looked, and thought the quiet of the scene
An emblem of the peace that yet shall be,
When o'er earth's continents, and isles between,
The noise of war shall cease from sea to sea,
And married nations dwell in harmony;
When millions, crouching in the dust to one,
No more shall beg their lives on bended knee,
Nor the black stake be dressed, nor in the sun
The o'erlabored captive toil, and wish his life were done.

Too long, at clash of arms amid her bowers
And pools of blood, the earth has stood aghast,

The fair earth, that should only blush with flowers
And ruddy fruits; but not for aye can last
The storm, and sweet the sunshine when 'tis past.
Lo, the clouds roll away—they break—they fly,
And, like the glorious light of summer, cast
O'er the wide landscape from the embracing sky,
On all the peaceful world the smile of heaven shall lie.

AUTUMN WOODS.

ERE, in the northern gale,
The summer tresses of the trees are gone,
The woods of Autumn, all around our vale,
Have put their glory on.

The mountains that infold,
In their wide sweep, the colored landscape round,
Seem groups of giant kings, in purple and gold,
That guard the enchanted ground.

I roam the woods that crown
The upland, where the mingled splendors glow,
Where the gay company of trees look down
On the green fields below.

My steps are not alone
In these bright walks; the sweet south-west, at play,
Flies, rustling, where the painted leaves are strown
Along the winding way.

And far in heaven, the while,
The sun, that sends that gale to wander here,
Pours out on the fair earth his quiet smile,—
The sweetest of the year.

Where now the solemn shade,
Verdure and gloom where many branches meet;
So grateful, when the noon of summer made
The valleys sick with heat?

Let in through all the trees
Come the strange rays; the forest depths are bright;
Their sunny-colored foliage, in the breeze,
Twinkles, like beams of light.

The rivulet, late unseen,
Where bickering through the shrubs its waters run,
Shines with the image of its golden screen
And glimmerings of the sun.

But, 'neath yon crimson tree,
Lover to listening maid might breathe his flame,
Nor mark, within its roseate canopy,
Her blush of maiden shame.

Oh, Autumn! why so soon
Depart the hues that make thy forests glad,
Thy gentle wind and thy fair sunny noon,
And leave thee wild and sad?

Ah! 'twere a lot too blest
For ever in thy colored shades to stray;
Amid the kisses of the soft south-west
To rove and dream for aye;

And leave the vain low strife
That makes men mad—the tug for wealth and power
The passions and the cares that wither life,
And waste its little hour.

NOVEMBER.

YET one smile more, departing, distant sun!
  One mellow smile through the soft vapory air,
Ere, o'er the frozen earth, the loud winds run,
  Or snows are sifted o'er the meadows bare.
One smile on the brown hills and naked trees,
  And the dark rocks whose summer wreaths are cast,
And the blue gentian flower, that, in the breeze,
  Nods lonely, of her beauteous race the last.
Yet a few sunny days, in which the bee
  Shall murmur by the hedge that skirts the way,
The cricket chirp upon the russet lea,
  And man delight to linger in thy ray.
Yet one rich smile, and we will try to bear
The piercing winter frost, and winds, and darkened air.

HYMN TO THE NORTH STAR.

THE sad and solemn night
  Hath yet her multitude of cheerful fires;
The glorious host of light
  Walk the dark hemisphere till she retires;
All through her silent watches, gliding slow,
Her constellations come, and climb the heavens, and go.

Day, too, hath many a star
To grace his gorgeous reign, as bright as they:
Through the blue fields afar,
Unseen, they follow in his flaming way:
Many a bright lingerer, as the eve grows dim,
Tells what a radiant troop arose and set with him.

And thou dost see them rise,
Star of the Pole! and thou dost see them set.
Alone, in thy cold skies,
Thou keep'st thy old unmoving station yet,
Nor join'st the dances of that glittering train,
Nor dipp'st thy virgin orb in the blue western main.

There, at morn's rosy birth,
Thou lookest meekly through the kindling air,
And eve, that round the earth
Chases the day, beholds thee watching there;
There noontide finds thee, and the hour that calls
The shapes of polar flame to scale heaven's azure walls.

Alike, beneath thine eye,
The deeds of darkness and of light are done;
High towards the star-lit sky
Towns blaze, the smoke of battle blots the sun,
The night-storm on a thousand hills is loud,
And the strong wind of day doth mingle sea and cloud.

On thy unaltering blaze
The half-wrecked mariner, his compass lost,
Fixes his steady gaze,
And steers, undoubting, to the friendly coast;
And they who stray in perilous wastes, by night,
Are glad when thou dost shine to guide their footsteps right.

And, therefore, bards of old,
Sages and hermits of the solemn wood,
Did in thy beams behold
A beauteous type of that unchanging good,
That bright eternal beacon, by whose ray
The voyager of time should shape his heedful way.

SONG OF THE STARS.

WHEN the radiant morn of creation broke,
And the world in the smile of God awoke,
And the empty realms of darkness and death
Were moved through their depths by his mighty breath,
And orbs of beauty and spheres of flame
From the void abyss by myriads came,—
In the joy of youth as they darted away,
Through the widening wastes of space to play,
Their silver voices in chorus rang,
And this was the song the bright ones sang:

"Away, away, through the wide, wide sky,
The fair blue fields that before us lie,—
Each sun with the worlds that round him roll,
Each planet, poised on her turning pole,
With her isles of green, and her clouds of white,
And her waters that lie like fluid light.

"For the source of glory uncovers his face,
And the brightness o'erflows unbounded space;
And we drink as we go the luminous tides
In our ruddy air and our blooming sides;
Lo, yonder the living splendors play;
Away, on our joyous path, away!

"Look, look, through our glittering ranks afar,
In the infinite azure, star after star,
How they brighten and bloom as they swiftly pass!
How the verdure runs o'er each rolling mass!
And the path of the gentle winds is seen,
Where the small waves dance, and the young woods lean.

"And see, where the brighter day-beams pour,
How the rainbows hang in the sunny shower;
And the morn and eve, with their pomp of hues,
Shift o'er the bright planets and shed their dews;
And 'twixt them both, o'er the teeming ground,
With her shadowy cone the night goes round!

"Away, away! in our blossoming bowers,
In the soft air wrapping these spheres of ours,
In the seas and fountains that shine with morn,
See, Love is brooding, and Life is born,
And breathing myriads are breaking from night,
To rejoice, like us, in motion and light.

"Glide on in your beauty, ye youthful spheres,
To weave the dance that measures the years;
Glide on, in the glory and gladness sent,
To the furthest wall of the firmament,—
The boundless visible smile of Him,
To the veil of whose brow your lamps are dim."

A FOREST HYMN.

THE groves were God's first temples. Ere man learned
To hew the shaft, and lay the architrave,
And spread the roof above them,—ere he framed
The lofty vault, to gather and roll back
The sound of anthems,—in the darkling wood,
Amid the cool and silence, he knelt down,
And offered to the Mightiest solemn thanks
And supplication. For his simple heart
Might not resist the sacred influences

Which, from the stilly twilight of the place,
And from the gray old trunks that high in heaven
Mingled their mossy boughs, and from the sound
Of the invisible breath that swayed at once
All their green tops, stole over him, and bowed
His spirit with the thought of boundless power
And inaccessible majesty. Ah, why
Should we, in the world's riper years, neglect
God's ancient sanctuaries, and adore
Only among the crowd, and under roofs
That our frail hands have raised? Let me, at least,
Here, in the shadow of this aged wood,
Offer one hymn—thrice happy, if it find
Acceptance in His ear.

Father, thy hand
Hath reared these venerable columns, thou
Didst weave this verdant roof. Thou didst look down
Upon the naked earth, and, forthwith, rose
All these fair ranks of trees. They, in thy sun,
Budded, and shook their green leaves in thy breeze,
And shot towards heaven. The century-living crow,
Whose birth was in their tops, grew old and died
Among their branches, till, at last, they stood,
As now they stand, massy, and tall, and dark,
Fit shrine for humble worshipper to hold
Communion with his Maker. These dim vaults,
These winding aisles, of human pomp or pride
Report not. No fantastic carvings show
The boast of our vain race to change the form
Of thy fair works. But thou art here—thou fill'st
The solitude. Thou art in the soft winds
That run along the summit of these trees

In music; thou art in the cooler breath
That from the inmost darkness of the place
Comes, scarcely felt; the barky trunks, the ground,
The fresh moist ground, are all instinct with thee.
Here is continual worship;—nature, here,
In the tranquillity that thou dost love,
Enjoys thy presence. Noiselessly, around,
From perch to perch, the solitary bird
Passes; and yon clear spring, that, midst its herbs,
Wells softly forth and wandering steeps the roots
Of half the mighty forest, tells no tale
Of all the good it does. Thou hast not left
Thyself without a witness, in these shades,
Of thy perfections. Grandeur, strength, and grace
Are here to speak of thee. This mighty oak—
By whose immovable stem I stand and seem
Almost annihilated—not a prince,
In all that proud old world beyond the deep,
E'er wore his crown as loftily as he
Wears the green coronal of leaves with which
Thy hand has graced him. Nestled at his root
Is beauty, such as blooms not in the glare
Of the broad sun. That delicate forest flower,
With scented breath, and look so like a smile,
Seems, as it issues from the shapeless mould,
An emanation of the indwelling Life,
A visible token of the upholding Love,
That are the soul of this wide universe.

My heart is awed within me when I think
Of the great miracle that still goes on,
In silence, round me—the perpetual work
Of thy creation, finished, yet renewed

For ever. Written on thy works I read
The lesson of thy own eternity.
Lo! all grow old and die—but see again,
How on the faltering footsteps of decay
Youth presses—ever gay and beautiful youth,
In all its beautiful forms. These lofty trees
Wave not less proudly that their ancestors
Moulder beneath them. Oh, there is not lost
One of earth's charms; upon her bosom yet,
After the flight of untold centuries,
The freshness of her far beginning lies
And yet shall lie. Life mocks the idle hate
Of his arch enemy Death—yea, seats himself
Upon the tyrant's throne—the sepulchre,
And of the triumphs of his ghastly foe
Makes his own nourishment. For he came forth
From thine own bosom, and shall have no end.

There have been holy men who hid themselves
Deep in the woody wilderness, and gave
Their lives to thought and prayer, till they outlived
The generation born with them, nor seemed
Less aged than the hoary trees and rocks
Around them;—and there have been holy men
Who deemed it were not well to pass life thus.
But let me often to these solitudes
Retire, and in thy presence reassure
My feeble virtue. Here its enemies,
The passions, at thy plainer footsteps shrink
And tremble and are still. Oh, God! when thou
Dost scare the world with tempests, set on fire
The heavens with falling thunderbolts, or fill
With all the waters of the firmament

The swift dark whirlwind that uproots the woods
And drowns the villages; when, at thy call,
Uprises the great deep and throws himself
Upon the continent, and overwhelms
Its cities—who forgets not, at the sight
Of these tremendous tokens of thy power,
His pride, and lays his strifes and follies by?
Oh, from these sterner aspects of thy face
Spare me and mine, nor let us need the wrath
Of the mad unchained elements to teach
Who rules them. Be it ours to meditate,
In these calm shades, thy milder majesty,
And to the beautiful order of thy works
Learn to conform the order of our lives.

"OH, FAIREST OF THE RURAL MAIDS."

OH, fairest of the rural maids!
Thy birth was in the forest shades;
Green boughs, and glimpses of the sky,
Were all that met thine infant eye.

Thy sports, thy wanderings, when a child,
Were ever in the sylvan wild;
And all the beauty of the place
Is in thy heart and on thy face.

The twilight of the trees and rocks
Is in the light shade of thy locks;
Thy step is as the wind, that weaves
Its playful way among the leaves.

Thine eyes are springs, in whose serene
And silent waters heaven is seen;
Their lashes are the herbs that look
On their young figures in the brook.

The forest depths, by foot unpressed,
Are not more sinless than thy breast;
The holy peace, that fills the air
Of those calm solitudes, is there.

LINES ON REVISITING THE COUNTRY.

I STAND upon my native hills again,
  Broad, round, and green, that in the summer sky,
With garniture of waving grass and grain,
  Orchards, and beechen forests, basking lie;
While deep the sunless glens are scooped between,
Where brawl o'er shallow beds the streams unseen.

A lisping voice and glancing eyes are near,
  And ever restless feet of one, who, now,
Gathers the blossoms of her fourth bright year;
  There plays a gladness o'er her fair young brow,
As breaks the varied scene upon her sight,
Upheaved and spread in verdure and in light.

For I have taught her, with delighted eye,
  To gaze upon the mountains,—to behold
With deep affection the pure ample sky,
  And clouds along its blue abysses rolled,—
To love the song of waters, and to hear
The melody of winds with charmed ear.

Here, I have 'scaped the city's stifling heat,
  Its horrid sounds, and its polluted air;
And, where the season's milder fervors beat,
  And gales, that sweep the forest borders, bear
The song of bird, and sound of running stream,
Am come awhile to wander and to dream.

Ay, flame thy fiercest, sun! thou canst not wake,
  In this pure air, the plague that walks unseen.
The maize leaf and the maple bough but take,
  From thy strong heats, a deeper, glossier green.
The mountain wind, that faints not in thy ray,
Sweeps the blue steams of pestilence away.

The mountain wind! most spiritual thing of all
  The wide earth knows; when, in the sultry time,
He stoops him from his vast cerulean hall,
  He seems the breath of a celestial clime!
As if from heaven's wide-open gates did flow
Health and refreshment on the world below.

THE DEATH OF THE FLOWERS.

THE melancholy days are come, the saddest of the year,
Of wailing winds, and naked woods, and meadows brown and sere.
Heaped in the hollows of the grove, the autumn leaves lie dead ;
They rustle to the eddying gust, and to the rabbit's tread.
The robin and the wren are flown, and from the shrubs the jay,
And from the wood-top calls the crow through all the gloomy day.

Where are the flowers, the fair young flowers, that lately sprang and stood
In brighter light, and softer airs, a beauteous sisterhood?
Alas ! they all are in their graves, the gentle race of flowers
Are lying in their lowly beds, with the fair and good of ours.
The rain is falling where they lie, but the cold November rain
Calls not from out the gloomy earth the lovely ones again.

The wind-flower and the violet, they perished long ago,
And the brier-rose and the orchis died amid the summer glow ;
But on the hill the golden-rod, and the aster in the wood,
And the yellow sun-flower by the brook, in autumn beauty stood,
Till fell the frost from the clear cold heaven, as falls the plague on men,
And the brightness of their smile was gone, from upland, glade, and glen.

And now, when comes the calm mild day, as still such days will come,
To call the squirrel and the bee from out their winter home ;

When the sound of dropping nuts is heard, though all the trees
are still,
And twinkle in the smoky light the waters of the rill,
The south wind searches for the flowers whose fragrance late
he bore,
And sighs to find them in the wood and by the stream nc
more.

And then I think of one who in her youthful beauty died,
The fair meek blossom that grew up and faded by my side;
In the cold moist earth we laid her, when the forest cast th
leaf,
And we wept that one so lovely should have a life so brief:
Yet not unmeet it was that one, like that young friend of ours,
So gentle and so beautiful, should perish with the flowers.

OCTOBER.

AY, thou art welcome, heaven's delicious breath,
When woods begin to wear the crimson leaf,
And suns grow meek, and the meek suns grow brief,
And the year smiles as it draws near its death.
Wind of the sunny south! oh, still delay
In the gay woods and in the golden air,
Like to a good old age released from care,
Journeying, in long serenity, away.
In such a bright, late quiet, would that I
Might wear out life like thee, mid bowers and brooks,
And, dearer yet, the sunshine of kind looks,
And music of kind voices ever nigh;
And when my last sand twinkled in the glass,
Pass silently from men, as thou dost pass.

THE GLADNESS OF NATURE.

IS this a time to be cloudy and sad,
  When our mother Nature laughs around;
When even the deep blue heavens look glad,
  And gladness breathes from the blossoming ground?

There are notes of joy from the hang-bird and wren,
And the gossip of swallows through all the sky;
The ground-squirrel gayly chirps by his den,
And the wilding bee hums merrily by.

The clouds are at play in the azure space,
And their shadows at play on the bright green vale,
And here they stretch to the frolic chase,
And there they roll on the easy gale.

There's a dance of leaves in that aspen bower,
There's a titter of winds in that beechen tree,
There's a smile on the fruit, and a smile on the flower,
And a laugh from the brook that runs to the sea.

And look at the broad-faced sun, how he smiles
On the dewy earth that smiles in his ray,
On the leaping waters and gay young isles;
Ay, look, and he'll smile thy gloom away.

MIDSUMMER.

A POWER is on the earth and in the air,
From which the vital spirit shrinks afraid,
And shelters him, in nooks of deepest shade,
From the hot steam and from the fiery glare.
Look forth upon the earth—her thousand plants
Are smitten; even the dark sun-loving maize
Faints in the field beneath the torrid blaze;
The herd beside the shaded fountain pants;

For life is driven from all the landscape brown ;
  The bird has sought his tree, the snake his den,
  The trout floats dead in the hot stream, and men
Drop by the sun-stroke in the populous town :
  As if the Day of Fire had dawned, and sent
  Its deadly breath into the firmament.

A SCENE ON THE BANKS OF THE HUDSON.

COOL shades and dews are round my way,
And silence of the early day;
Mid the dark rocks that watch his bed,
Glitters the mighty Hudson spread,
Unrippled, save by drops that fall
From shrubs that fringe his mountain wall;
And o'er the clear still water swells
The music of the Sabbath bells.

All, save this little nook of land,
Circled with trees, on which I stand;
All, save that line of hills which lie
Suspended in the mimic sky—
Seems a blue void, above, below,
Through which the white clouds come and go
And from the green world's farthest steep
I gaze into the airy deep.

Loveliest of lovely things are they,
On earth, that soonest pass away.
The rose that lives its little hour
Is prized beyond the sculptured flower.
Even love, long tried and cherished long,
Becomes more tender and more strong,
At thought of that insatiate grave
From which its yearnings cannot save.

River! in this still hour thou hast
Too much of heaven on earth to last;
Nor long may thy still waters lie,
An image of the glorious sky.
Thy fate and mine are not repose,
And ere another evening close,
Thou to thy tides shalt turn again,
And I to seek the crowd of men.

THE EVENING WIND.

SPIRIT that breathest through my lattice, thou
That cool'st the twilight of the sultry day,
Gratefully flows thy freshness round my brow;
Thou hast been out upon the deep at play,
Riding all day the wild blue waves till now,
Roughening their crests, and scattering high their spray,
And swelling the white sail. I welcome thee
To the scorched land, thou wanderer of the sea!

Nor I alone—a thousand bosoms round
Inhale thee in the fulness of delight;
And languid forms rise up, and pulses bound
Livelier, at coming of the wind of night;
And, languishing to hear thy grateful sound,
Lies the vast inland stretched beyond the sight.
Go forth into the gathering shade; go forth,
God's blessing breathed upon the fainting earth!

Go, rock the little wood-bird in his nest,
  Curl the still waters, bright with stars, and rouse
The wide old wood from his majestic rest,
  Summoning from the innumerable boughs
The strange, deep harmonies that haunt his breast:
  Pleasant shall be thy way where meekly bows
The shutting flower, and darkling waters pass,
And where the o'ershadowing branches sweep the grass.

The faint old man shall lean his silver head
  To feel thee; thou shalt kiss the child asleep,
And dry the moistened curls that overspread
  His temples, while his breathing grows more deep;
And they who stand about the sick man's bed,
  Shall joy to listen to thy distant sweep,
And softly part his curtains to allow
Thy visit, grateful to his burning brow.

Go—but the circle of eternal change,
  Which is the life of nature, shall restore,
With sounds and scents from all thy mighty range,
  Thee to thy birthplace of the deep once more;
Sweet odors in the sea-air, sweet and strange,
  Shall tell the homesick mariner of the shore;
And, listening to thy murmur, he shall deem
He hears the rustling leaf and running stream.

TO THE FRINGED GENTIAN.

THOU blossom bright with autumn dew,
And colored with the heaven's own blue,
That openest when the quiet light
Succeeds the keen and frosty night—

Thou comest not when violets lean
O'er wandering brooks and springs unseen,
Or columbines, in purple dressed,
Nod o'er the ground-bird's hidden nest.

Thou waitest late and com'st alone,
When woods are bare and birds are flown,
And frosts and shortening days portend
The aged year is near his end.

Then doth thy sweet and quiet eye
Look through its fringes to the sky,
Blue—blue—as if that sky let fall
A flower from its cerulean wall.

I would that thus, when I shall see
The hour of death draw near to me,
Hope, blossoming within my heart,
May look to heaven as I depart.

A SUMMER RAMBLE.

THE quiet August noon has come,
  A slumberous silence fills the sky,
The fields are still, the woods are dumb,
  In glassy sleep the waters lie.

And mark yon soft white clouds that rest
  Above our vale, a moveless throng ;
The cattle on the mountain's breast
  Enjoy the grateful shadow long.

Oh, how unlike those merry hours,
  In early June, when Earth laughs out,
When the fresh winds make love to flowers,
  And woodlands sing and waters shout;

When in the grass sweet voices talk,
  And strains of tiny music swell
From every moss cup of the rock,
  From every nameless blossom's bell.

But now a joy too deep for sound,
  A peace no other season knows,
Hushes the heavens and wraps the ground,
  The blessing of supreme repose.

Away! I will not be, to-day,
  The only slave of toil and care.
Away from desk and dust! away!
  I'll be as idle as the air.

Beneath the open sky abroad,
  Among the plants and breathing things,
The sinless, peaceful works of God,
  I'll share the calm the season brings.

Come, thou, in whose soft eyes I see
  The gentle meanings of thy heart,
One day amid the woods with me,
  From men and all their cares apart.

And where, upon the meadow's breast,
The shadow of the thicket lies,
The blue wild flowers thou gatherest
Shall glow yet deeper near thine eyes.

Come, and when, mid the calm profound,
I turn, those gentle eyes to seek,
They, like the lovely landscape round,
Of innocence and peace shall speak.

Rest here, beneath the unmoving shade,
And on the silent valleys gaze,
Winding and widening, till they fade
In yon soft ring of summer haze.

The village trees their summits rear
Still as its spire, and yonder flock,
At rest in those calm fields, appear
As chiselled from the lifeless rock.

One tranquil mount the scene o'erlooks—
There the hushed winds their sabbath keep,
While a near hum from bees and brooks
Comes faintly like the breath of sleep.

Well may the gazer deem that when,
Worn with the struggle and the strife,
And heart-sick at the wrongs of men,
The good forsakes the scene of life;

Like this deep quiet that, awhile,
Lingers the lovely landscape o'er,
Shall be the peace whose holy smile
Welcomes him to a happier shore.

CATTERSKILL FALLS.

MIDST greens and shades the Catterskill leaps,
  From cliffs where the wood-flower clings ;
All summer he moistens his verdant steeps
  With the sweet light spray of the mountain springs ;
And he shakes the woods on the mountain side,
When they drip with the rains of autumn-tide.

But when, in the forest bare and old,
  The blast of December calls,
He builds, in the starlight clear and cold,
  A palace of ice where his torrent falls,
With turret, and arch, and fretwork fair.
And pillars blue as the summer air.

For whom are those glorious chambers wrought,
  In the cold and cloudless night?
Is there neither spirit nor motion of thought
  In forms so lovely and hues so bright?
Hear what the gray-haired woodmen tell
Of this wild stream and its rocky dell.

'Twas hither a youth of dreamy mood,
  A hundred winters ago,
Had wandered over the mighty wood,
  When the panther's track was fresh on the snow,
And keen were the winds that came to stir
The long dark boughs of the hemlock-fir.

Too gentle of mien he seemed and fair
  For a child of those rugged steeps;
His home lay low in the valley where
  The kingly Hudson rolls to the deeps;
But he wore the hunter's frock that day,
And a slender gun on his shoulder lay.

And here he paused, and against the trunk
  Of a tall gray linden leant,
When the broad clear orb of the sun had sunk
  From his path in the frosty firmament,
And over the round dark edge of the hill
A cold green light was quivering still.

And the crescent moon, high over the green,
  From a sky of crimson shone
On that icy palace, whose towers were seen
  To sparkle as if with stars of their own;
While the water fell with a hollow sound,
'Twixt the glistening pillars ranged around.

Is that a being of life, that moves
  Where the crystal battlements rise?
A maiden watching the moon she loves,
  At the twilight hour, with pensive eyes?
Was that a garment which seemed to gleam
Betwixt his eye and the falling stream?

'Tis only the torrent tumbling o'er,
  In the midst of those glassy walls,
Gushing, and plunging, and beating the floor
  Of the rocky basin in which it falls.
'Tis only the torrent—but why that start?
Why gazes the youth with a throbbing heart?

He thinks no more of his home afar,
  Where his sire and sister wait.
He heeds no longer how star after stat
  Looks forth on the night as the hour grows late.
He heeds not the snow-wreaths, lifted and cast
From a thousand boughs by the rising blast.

His thoughts are alone of those who dwell
  In the halls of frost and snow,
Who pass where the crystal domes upswell
  From the alabaster floors below,
Where the frost-trees shoot with leaf and spray,
And frost-gems scatter a silvery day.

"And oh, that those glorious haunts were mine!"
  He speaks, and throughout the glen
Thin shadows swim in the faint moonshine,
  And take a ghastly likeness of men,
As if the slain by the wintry storms
Came forth to the air in their earthly forms.

There pass the chasers of seal and whale,
  With their weapons quaint and grim,
And bands of warriors in glittering mail,
  And herdsmen and hunters huge of limb;
There are naked arms, with bow and spear,
And furry gauntlets the carbine rear.

There are mothers—and oh, how sadly their eyes
  On their children's white brows rest!
There are youthful lovers—the maiden lies,
  In a seeming sleep, on the chosen breast;
There are fair wan women with moonstruck air,
The snow-stars flecking their long loose hair

They eye him not as they pass along,
  But his hair stands up with dread,
When he feels that he moves with that phantom throng,
  Till those icy turrets are over his head,
And the torrent's roar as they enter seems
Like a drowsy murmur heard in dreams.

The glittering threshold is scarcely passed,
  When there gathers and wraps him round
A thick white twilight, sullen and vast,
  In which there is neither form nor sound;
The phantoms, the glory, vanish all,
With the dying voice of the waterfall.

Slow passes the darkness of that trance,
  And the youth now faintly sees
Huge shadows and gushes of light that dance
  On a rugged ceiling of unhewn trees,
And walls where the skins of beasts are hung,
And rifles glitter on antlers strung.

On a couch of shaggy skins he lies;
  As he strives to raise his head,
Hard-featured woodmen, with kindly eyes,
  Come round him and smooth his furry bed,
And bid him rest, for the evening star
Is scarcely set and the day is far.

They had found at eve the dreaming one
  By the base of that icy steep,
When over his stiffening limbs begun
  The deadly slumber of frost to creep,
And they cherished the pale and breathless form.
Till the stagnant blood ran free and warm.

"EARTH'S CHILDREN CLEAVE TO EARTH."

EARTH'S children cleave to Earth—her frail
  Decaying children dread decay.
Yon wreath of mist that leaves the vale,
  And lessens in the morning ray;
Look, how, by mountain rivulet,
  It lingers as it upward creeps,
And clings to fern and copsewood set
  Along the green and dewy steeps;
Clings to the flowery kalmia, clings
  To precipices fringed with grass,
Dark maples where the wood-thrush sings,
  And bowers of fragrant sassafras.
Yet all in vain—it passes still
  From hold to hold; it cannot stay,
And in the very beams that fill
  The world with glory, wastes away,
Till, parting from the mountain's brow,
  It vanishes from human eye,
And that which sprung of earth is now
  A portion of the glorious sky.

THE WINDS.

I.

YE winds, ye unseen currents of the air,
  Softly ye played a few brief hours ago;
Ye bore the murmuring bee; ye tossed the hair
  O'er maiden cheeks, that took a fresher glow;

Ye rolled the round white cloud through depths of blue
Ye shook from shaded flowers the lingering dew;
Before you the catalpa's blossoms flew,
  Light blossoms, dropping on the grass like snow.

II.

How are ye changed! Ye take the cataract's sound
  Ye take the whirlpool's fury and its might;
The mountain shudders as ye sweep the ground;
  The valley woods lie prone beneath your flight.
The clouds before you shoot like eagles past;
The homes of men are rocking in your blast;
Ye lift the roofs like autumn leaves, and cast,
  Skyward, the whirling fragments out of sight.

III.

The weary fowls of heaven make wing in vain,
  To escape your wrath; ye seize and dash them dead
Against the earth ye drive the roaring rain;
  The harvest-field becomes a river's bed;
And torrents tumble from the hills around,
Plains turn to lakes, and villages are drowned,
And wailing voices, midst the tempest's sound,
  Rise, as the rushing waters swell and spread.

IV.

Ye dart upon the deep, and straight is heard
  A wilder roar, and men grow pale, and pray;
Ye fling its floods around you, as a bird
  Flings o'er his shivering plumes the fountain's spray.

See! to the breaking mast the sailor clings;
Ye scoop the ocean to its briny springs,
And take the mountain billow on your wings,
  And pile the wreck of navies round the bay.

V.

Why rage ye thus?—no strife for liberty
  Has made you mad; no tyrant, strong through fear,
Has chained your pinions till ye wrenched them free,
  And rushed into the unmeasured atmosphere;
For ye were born in freedom where ye blow;
Free o'er the mighty deep to come and go;
Earth's solemn woods were yours, her wastes of snow,
  Her isles where summer blossoms all the year.

VI.

O ye wild winds! a mightier Power than yours
  In chains upon the shore of Europe lies;
The sceptred throng, whose fetters he endures,
  Watch his mute throes with terror in their eyes:
And armed warriors all around him stand,
And, as he struggles, tighten every band,
And lift the heavy spear, with threatening hand,
  To pierce the victim, should he strive to rise.

VII.

Yet oh, when that wronged Spirit of our race
  Shall break, as soon he must, his long-worn chains,
And leap in freedom from his prison-place,
  Lord of his ancient hills and fruitful plains,

Let him not rise, like these mad winds of air,
To waste the loveliness that time could spare,
To fill the earth with wo, and blot her fair
Unconscious breast with blood from human veins.

VIII.

But may he like the spring-time come abroad,
Who crumbles winter's gyves with gentle might,
When in the genial breeze, the breath of God,
Come spouting up the unsealed springs to light;
Flowers start from their dark prisons at his feet;
The woods, long dumb, awake to hymnings sweet,
And morn and eve, whose glimmerings almost meet,
Crowd back to narrow bounds the ancient night.

THE PAINTED CUP.

THE fresh savannas of the Sangamon
Here rise in gentle swells, and the long grass
Is mixed with rustling hazels. Scarlet tufts
Are glowing in the green, like flakes of fire;
The wanderers of the prairie know them well,
And call that brilliant flower the Painted Cup.

Now, if thou art a poet, tell me not
That these bright chalices were tinted thus
To hold the dew for fairies, when they meet
On moonlight evenings in the hazel bowers,
And dance till they are thirsty. Call not up,
Amid this fresh and virgin solitude,

The faded fancies of an elder world;
But leave these scarlet cups to spotted moths
Of June, and glistening flies, and humming-birds,
To drink from, when on all these boundless lawns
The morning sun looks hot. Or let the wind
O'erturn in sport their ruddy brims, and pour
A sudden shower upon the strawberry plant,
To swell the reddening fruit that even now
Breathes a slight fragrance from the sunny slope.

But thou art of a gayer fancy. Well—
Let then the gentle Manitou of flowers,
Lingering amid the bloomy waste he loves,
Though all his swarthy worshippers are gone—
Slender and small, his rounded cheek all brown
And ruddy with the sunshine; let him come
On summer mornings, when the blossoms wake,
And part with little hands the spiky grass;
And touching, with his cherry lips, the edge
Of these bright beakers, drain the gathered dew.

A HYMN OF THE SEA.

THE sea is mighty, but a mightier sways
His restless billows. Thou, whose hands have scooped
His boundless gulfs and built his shore, thy breath,
That moved in the beginning o'er his face,
Moves o'er it evermore. The obedient waves

To its strong motion roll, and rise and fall.
Still from that realm of rain thy cloud goes up,
As at the first, to water the great earth,
And keep her valleys green. A hundred realms
Watch its broad shadow warping on the wind,
And in the dropping shower, with gladness hear
Thy promise of the harvest. I look forth
Over the boundless blue, where joyously
The bright crests of innumerable waves
Glance to the sun at once, as when the hands
Of a great multitude are upward flung
In acclamation. I behold the ships
Gliding from cape to cape, from isle to isle,
Or stemming toward far lands, or hastening home
From the old world. It is thy friendly breeze
That bears them, with the riches of the land,
And treasure of dear lives, till, in the port,
The shouting seaman climbs and furls the sail.

But who shall bide thy tempest, who shall face
The blast that wakes the fury of the sea?
Oh God! thy justice makes the world turn pale,
When on the armed fleet, that royally
Bears down the surges, carrying war, to smite
Some city, or invade some thoughtless realm,
Descends the fierce tornado. The vast hulks
Are whirled like chaff upon the waves; the sails
Fly, rent like webs of gossamer; the masts
Are snapped asunder; downward from the decks,
Downward are slung, into the fathomless gulf,
Their cruel engines; and their hosts, arrayed
In trappings of the battle-field, are whelmed
By whirlpools, or dashed dead upon the rocks.

Then stand the nations still with awe, and pause,
A moment, from the bloody work of war.

These restless surges eat away the shores
Of earth's old continents; the fertile plain
Welters in shallows, headlands crumble down,
And the tide drifts the sea-sand in the streets
Of the drowned city. Thou, meanwhile, afar
In the green chambers of the middle sea,
Where broadest spread the waters and the line
Sinks deepest, while no eye beholds thy work
Creator! thou dost teach the coral worm
To lay his mighty reefs. From age to age,
He builds beneath the waters, till, at last,
His bulwarks overtop the brine, and check
The long wave rolling from the southern pole
To break upon Japan. Thou bidd'st the fires
That smoulder under ocean, heave on high
The new-made mountains, and uplift their peaks,
A place of refuge for the storm-driven bird.
The birds and wafting billows plant the rifts
With herb and tree; sweet fountains gush; sweet airs
Ripple the living lakes that, fringed with flowers,
Are gathered in the hollows. Thou dost look
On thy creation and pronounce it good.
Its valleys, glorious with their summer green,
Praise thee in silent beauty, and its woods,
Swept by the murmuring winds of ocean, join
The murmuring shores in a perpetual hymn.

THE UNKNOWN WAY.

A BURNING sky is o'er me,
  The sands beneath me glow,
As onward, onward, wearily,
  In the sultry noon I go.

From the dusty path there opens,
  Eastward, an unknown way ;
Above its windings, pleasantly,
  The woodland branches play.

A silvery brook comes stealing
  From the shadow of its trees,
Where slender herbs of the forest stoop
  Before the entering breeze.

Along those pleasant windings
  I would my journey lay,
Where the shade is cool and the dew of night
  Is not yet dried away.

Path of the flowery woodland !
  Oh whither dost thou lead,
Wandering by grassy orchard grounds
  Or by the open mead ?

Goest thou by nestling cottage ?
  Goest thou by stately hall,
Where the broad elm droops, a leafy dome,
  And woodbines flaunt on the wall ?

By steeps where children gather
  Flowers of the yet fresh year?
By lonely walks where lovers stray
  Till the tender stars appear?

Or haply dost thou linger
  On barren plains and bare,
Or clamber the bald mountain side
  Into the thinner air?

Where they who journey upward
  Walk in a weary track,
And oft upon the shady vale
  With longing eyes look back?

I hear a solemn murmur,
  And, listening to the sound,
I know the voice of the mighty sea,
  Beating his pebbly bound.

Dost thou, oh path of the woodland!
  End where those waters roar,
Like human life, on a trackless beach,
  With a boundless Sea before?

THE PLANTING OF THE APPLE TREE.

COME, let us plant the apple tree.
Cleave the tough greensward with the spade
Wide let its hollow bed be made;
There gently lay the roots, and there
Sift the dark mould with kindly care,

And press it o'er them tenderly,
As round the sleeping infant's feet
We softly fold the cradle sheet;
So plant we the apple tree.

What plant we in this apple tree?
Buds, which the breath of summer days
Shall lengthen into leafy sprays;
Boughs where the thrush, with crimson breast,
Shall haunt and sing and hide her nest;
We plant, upon the sunny lea,
A shadow for the noontide hour,
A shelter from the summer shower,
When we plant the apple tree.

What plant we in this apple tree?
Sweets for a hundred flowery springs,
To load the May-wind's restless wings,
When, from the orchard row, he pours
Its fragrance through our open doors;
A world of blossoms for the bee,
Flowers for the sick girl's silent room,
For the glad infant sprigs of bloom,
We plant with the apple tree.

What plant we in this apple tree?
Fruits that shall swell in sunny June,
And redden in the August noon,
And drop, when gentle airs come by,
That fan the blue September sky,
While children come, with cries of glee,
And seek them where the fragrant grass
Betrays their bed to those who pass,
At the foot of the apple tree.

And when, above this apple tree,
The winter stars are quivering bright,
And winds go howling through the night,
Girls, whose young eyes o'erflow with mirth,
Shall peel its fruit by cottage hearth;
And guests in prouder homes shall see,
Heaped with the grape of Cintra's vine,
And golden orange of the line,
The fruit of the apple tree.

The fruitage of this apple tree
Winds and our flag of stripe and star
Shall bear to coasts that lie afar,
Where men shall wonder at the view,
And ask in what fair groves they grew;
And sojourners beyond the sea
Shall think of childhood's careless day,
And long, long hours of summer play,
In the shade of the apple tree.

Each year shall give this apple tree
A broader flush of roseate bloom,
A deeper maze of verdurous gloom,
And loosen, when the frost-clouds lower,
The crisp brown leaves in thicker shower.
The years shall come and pass, but we
Shall hear no longer, where we lie,
The summer's songs, the autumn's sigh,
In the boughs of the apple tree.

And time shall waste this apple tree.
Oh, when its aged branches throw
Thin shadows on the ground below,

Shall fraud and force and iron will
Oppress the weak and helpless still?
 What shall the tasks of mercy be,
Amid the toils, the strifes, the tears,
Of those who live when length of years
 Is wasting this apple tree?

 "Who planted this old apple tree?"
The children of that distant day
Thus to some aged man shall say;
And gazing on its mossy stem,
The gray-haired man shall answer them:
 "A poet of the land was he,
Born in the rude but good old times;
'Tis said he made some quaint old rhymes
 On planting the apple tree."

ROBERT OF LINCOLN.

MERRILY swinging on brier and weed,
 Near to the nest of his little dame,
Over the mountain-side or mead,
 Robert of Lincoln is telling his name:
 Bob-o'-link, bob-o'-link,
 Spink, spank, spink;
Snug and safe is that nest of ours,
Hidden among the summer flowers.
 Chee, chee, chee.

Robert of Lincoln is gayly drest,
   Wearing a bright black wedding coat;
White are his shoulders and white his crest,
   Hear him call in his merry note:
      Bob-o'-link, bob-o'-link,
      Spink, spank, spink;
Look what a nice new coat is mine,
Sure there was never a bird so fine.
            Chee, chee, chee.

Robert of Lincoln's Quaker wife,
   Pretty and quiet, with plain brown wings,
Passing at home a patient life,
   Broods in the grass while her husband sings
      Bob-o'-link, bob-o'-link,
      Spink, spank, spink;
Brood, kind creature; you need not fear
Thieves and robbers while I am here.
            Chee, chee, chee.

Modest and shy as a nun is she;
   One weak chirp is her only note.
Braggart and prince of braggarts is he,
   Pouring boasts from his little throat:
      Bob-o'-link, bob-o'-link,
      Spink, spank, spink;
Never was I afraid of man;
Catch me, cowardly knaves, if you can.
            Chee, chee, chee.

Six white eggs on a bed of hay,
   Flecked with purple, a pretty sight!

There as the mother sits all day,
   Robert is singing with all his might
      Bob-o'-link, bob-o'-link,
      Spink, spank, spink;
Nice, good wife, that never goes out,
Keeping house while I frolic about.
            Chee, chee, chee.

Soon as the little ones chip the shell,
   Six wide mouths are open for food;
Robert of Lincoln bestirs him well,
   Gathering seeds for the hungry brood.
      Bob-o'-link, bob-o'-link,
      Spink, spank, spink;
This new life is likely to be
Hard for a gay young fellow like me.
            Chee, chee, chee.

Robert of Lincoln at length is made
   Sober with work, and silent with care;
Off is his holiday garment laid,
   Half forgotten that merry air:
      Bob-o'-link, bob-o'-link,
      Spink, spank, spink;
Nobody knows but my mate and I
Where our nest and our nestlings lie.
            Chee, chee, chee.

Summer wanes; the children are grown;
   Fun and frolic no more he knows;
Robert of Lincoln's a humdrum crone;
   Off he flies, and we sing as he goes:

Bob-o'-link, bob-o'-link,
Spink, spank, spink;
When you can pipe that merry old strain,
Robert of Lincoln, come back again.
Chee, chee, chee.

AN INVITATION TO THE COUNTRY.

ALREADY, close by our summer dwelling,
The Easter sparrow repeats her song;
A merry warbler, she chides the blossoms—
The idle blossoms that sleep so long.

The blue-bird chants, from the elm's long branches,
A hymn to welcome the budding year.
The south wind wanders from field to forest,
And softly whispers: The Spring is here.

Come, daughter mine, from the gloomy city,
Before those lays from the elm have ceased;
The violet breathes, by our door, as sweetly
As in the air of her native East.

Though many a flower in the wood is waking,
The daffodil is our doorside queen;
She pushes upward the sward already,
To spot with sunshine the early green.

No lays so joyous as these are warbled
From wiry prison in maiden's bower;
No pampered bloom of the greenhouse chamber
Has half the charm of the lawn's first flower.

Yet these sweet sounds of the early season,
And these fair sights of its sunny days,
Are only sweet when we fondly listen,
And only fair when we fondly gaze.

There is no glory in star or blossom,
Till looked upon by a loving eye;
There is no fragrance in April breezes,
Till breathed with joy as they wander by.

Come, Julia dear, for the sprouting willows,
The opening flowers, and the gleaming brooks,
And hollows, green in the sun, are waiting
Their dower of beauty from thy glad looks.

THE SONG OF THE SOWER.

I.

THE maples redden in the sun;
  In autumn gold the beeches stand;
Rest, faithful plough, thy work is done
    Upon the teeming land.
Bordered with trees whose gay leaves fly
On every breath that sweeps the sky,
The fresh dark acres furrowed lie,
    And ask the sower's hand.
Loose the tired steer and let him go
To pasture where the gentians blow,
And we, who till the grateful ground,
Fling we the golden shower around.

II.

Fling wide the generous grain; we fling
O'er the dark mould the green of spring.
For thick the emerald blades shall grow,
When first the March winds melt the snow,
And to the sleeping flowers, below,
    The early bluebirds sing.
Fling wide the grain; we give the fields
  The ears that nod in summer's gale,
The shining stems that summer gilds,
  The harvest that o'erflows the vale,
And swells, an amber sea, between
The full-leaved woods, its shores of green.

Hark! from the murmuring clods I hear
Glad voices of the coming year;
The song of him who binds the grain,
The shout of those that load the wain,
And from the distant grange there comes
  The clatter of the thresher's flail,
And steadily the millstone hums
  Down in the willowy vale.

III.

Fling wide the golden shower; we trust
The strength of armies to the dust;
This peaceful lea may haply yield
Its harvest for the tented field.
Ha! feel ye not your fingers thrill,
  As o'er them, in the yellow grains,
Glide the warm drops of blood that fill,
  For mortal strife, the warrior's veins;
Such as, on Solferino's day,
Slaked the brown sand and flowed away;—
Flowed till the herds, on Mincio's brink,
Snuffed the red stream and feared to drink;—
Blood that in deeper pools shall lie
  On the sad earth, as time grows gray,
When men by deadlier arts shall die,
And deeper darkness blot the sky
    Above the thundering fray;
And realms, that hear the battle cry,
    Shall sicken with dismay;
And chieftains to the war shall lead
Whole nations, with the tempest's speed,
    To perish in a day;—

Till man, by love and mercy taught,
Shall rue the wreck his fury wrought,
And lay the sword away.
Oh strew, with pausing, shuddering hand,
The seed upon the helpless land,
As if, at every step, ye cast
The pelting hail and riving blast.

IV.

Nay, strew, with free and joyous sweep,
The seed upon the expecting soil;
For hence the plenteous year shall heap
The garners of the men who toil.
Strew the bright seed for those who tear
The matted sward with spade and share,
And those whose sounding axes gleam
Beside the lonely forest stream,
Till its broad banks lie bare;
And him who breaks the quarry-ledge,
With hammer-blows, plied quick and strong,
And him who, with the steady sledge,
Smites the shrill anvil all day long.
Sprinkle the furrow's even trace
For those whose toiling hands uprear
The roof-trees of our swarming race,
By grove and plain, by stream and mere;
Who forth, from crowded city, lead
The lengthening street, and overlay
Green orchard plot and grassy mead
With pavement of the murmuring way.
Cast, with full hands, the harvest cast,
For the brave men that climb the mast,

When to the billow and the blast
  It swings and stoops, with fearful strain,
And bind the fluttering mainsail fast,
  Till the tossed bark shall sit, again,
  Safe as a seabird in the main.

V.

Fling wide the grain for those who throw
The clanking shuttle to and fro,
In the long row of humming rooms,
  And into ponderous masses wind
The web that, from a thousand looms,
    Comes forth to clothe mankind.
Strew, with free sweep, the grain for them,
    By whom the busy thread
Along the garment's even hem
    And winding seam is led;
A pallid sisterhood, that keep
    The lonely lamp alight,
In strife with weariness and sleep,
    Beyond the middle night.
Large part be theirs in what the year
Shall ripen for the reaper here.

VI.

Still strew, with joyous hand, the wheat
On the soft mould beneath our feet;
    For even now I seem
To hear a sound that lightly rings
From murmuring harp and viol's strings,
    As in a summer dream.

The welcome of the wedding guest,
  The bridegroom's look of bashful pride,
  The faint smile of the pallid bride,
And bridemaid's blush at matron's jest,
And dance and song and generous dower,
Are in the shining grains we shower.

VII.

Scatter the wheat for shipwrecked men,
Who, hunger-worn, rejoice again
  In the sweet safety of the shore,
And wanderers, lost in woodlands drear,
Whose pulses bound with joy to hear
  The herd's light bell once more.
  Freely the golden spray be shed
For him whose heart, when night comes down
On the close alleys of the town,
  Is faint for lack of bread.
In chill roof chambers, bleak and bare,
Or the damp cellar's stifling air,
She who now sees, in mute despair,
    Her children pine for food,
Shall feel the dews of gladness start
To lids long tearless, and shall part
The sweet loaf, with a grateful heart,
    Among her thin, pale brood.
Dear, kindly Earth, whose breast we till!
Oh, for thy famished children, fill,
    Where'er the sower walks,
Fill the rich ears that shade the mould
With grain for grain, a hundredfold,
    To bend the sturdy stalks.

VIII.

Strew silently the fruitful seed,
As softly o'er the tilth ye tread,
For hands that delicately knead
The consecrated bread,
The mystic loaf that crowns the board,
When, round the table of their Lord,
Within a thousand temples set,
In memory of the bitter death
Of Him who taught at Nazareth,
His followers are met,
And thoughtful eyes with tears are wet,
As of the Holy One they think,
The glory of whose rising yet
Makes bright the grave's mysterious brink.

IX.

Brethren, the sower's task is done;
The seed is in its winter bed.
Now let the dark brown mould be spread,
To hide it from the sun,
And leave it to the kindly care
Of the still earth and brooding air;
As when the mother, from her breast,
Lays the hushed babe apart to rest,
And shades its eyes and waits to see
How sweet its waking smile will be.
The tempest now may smite, the sleet
All night on the drowned furrow beat,
And winds that, from the cloudy hold

Of winter, breathe the bitter cold,
Stiffen to stone the mellow mould,
　Yet safe shall lie the wheat:
Till, out of heaven's unmeasured blue,
　Shall walk again the genial year,
To wake with warmth and nurse with dew
　The germs we lay to slumber here.

X.

Oh blessed harvest yet to be!
　Abide thou with the love that keeps,
In its warm bosom, tenderly,
　The life which wakes and that which sleeps.
The love that leads the willing spheres
Along the unending track of years,
And watches o'er the sparrow's nest,
Shall brood above thy winter rest,
And raise thee from the dust, to hold
　Light whisperings with the winds of May,
And fill thy spikes with living gold,
　From summer's yellow ray.
Then, as thy garners give thee forth,
　On what glad errands shalt thou go,
Wherever, o'er the waiting earth,
　Roads wind and rivers flow.
The ancient East shall welcome thee
To mighty marts beyond the sea,
And they who dwell where palm groves sound
To summer winds the whole year round,
Shall watch, in gladness, from the shore,
The sails that bring thy glittering store.

THE NEW AND THE OLD.

NEW are the leaves on the oaken spray,
New the blades of the silky grass;
Flowers, that were buds but yesterday,
Peep from the ground where'er I pass.

These gay idlers, the butterflies,
Broke, to-day, from their winter shroud;
These soft airs, that winnow the skies,
Blow, just born, from the soft, white cloud.

Gushing fresh in the little streams,
What a prattle the waters make!
Even the sun, with his tender beams,
Seems as young as the flowers they wake.

Children are wading, with cheerful cries,
In the shoals of the sparkling brook;
Laughing maidens, with soft, young eyes,
Walk or sit in the shady nook.

What am I doing, thus alone,
In the glory of nature here,
Silver-haired, like a snow-flake thrown
On the greens of the springing year?

Only for brows unploughed by care,
Eyes that glisten with hope and mirth,
Cheeks unwrinkled, and unblanched hair,
Shines this holiday of the earth.

Under the grass, with the clammy clay,
  Lie in darkness the last year's flowers,
Born of a light that has passed away,
  Dews long dried, and forgotten showers.

"Under the grass is the fitting home,"
  So they whisper, "for such as thou,
When the winter of life is come,
  Chilling the blood, and frosting the brow."

THE THIRD OF NOVEMBER, 1861.

SOFTLY breathes the west wind beside the ruddy forest,
  Taking leaf by leaf from the branches where he flies.
Sweetly streams the sunshine, this third day of November,
  Through the golden haze of the quiet autumn skies.

Tenderly the season has spared the grassy meadows,
  Spared the petted flowers that the old world gave the new,
Spared the autumn rose and the garden's group of pansies,
  Late-blown dandelions and periwinkles blue.

On my cornice linger the ripe black grapes ungathered;
  Children fill the groves with the echoes of their glee,
Gathering tawny chestnuts, and shouting when beside them
  Drops the heavy fruit of the tall black-walnut tree.

Glorious are the woods in their latest gold and crimson,
  Yet our full-leaved willows are in their freshest green.
Such a kindly autumn, so mercifully dealing
  With the growths of summer, I never yet have seen.

Like this kindly season may life's decline come o'er me;
  Past is manhood's summer, the frosty months are here;
Yet be genial airs and a pleasant sunshine left me,
  Leaf, and fruit, and blossom, to mark the closing year.

Dreary is the time when the flowers of earth are withered ;
  Dreary is the time when the woodland leaves are cast,
When, upon the hillside, all hardened into iron,
  Howling, like a wolf, flies the famished northern blast.

Dreary are the years when the eye can look no longer
  With delight on nature, or hope on human kind ;
Oh may those that whiten my temples, as they pass me
  Leave the heart unfrozen, and spare the cheerful mind.

HUMOROUS POEMS.

BY

OLIVER WENDELL HOLMES.

WITH ILLUSTRATIONS BY SOL EYTINGE, JR.

BOSTON:
FIELDS, OSGOOD, & CO.,
SUCCESSORS TO TICKNOR AND FIELDS.
1869.

UNIVERSITY PRESS: WELCH, BIGELOW, & Co.,
CAMBRIDGE.

The River Darkies.

HUMOROUS POEMS.

THE BALLAD OF THE OYSTERMAN.

IT was a tall young oysterman lived by the river-side,
His shop was just upon the bank, his boat was on the tide;
The daughter of a fisherman, that was so straight and slim,
Lived over on the other bank, right opposite to him.

It was the pensive oysterman that saw a lovely maid,
Upon a moonlight evening, a sitting in the shade;
He saw her wave her handkerchief, as much as if to say,
"I 'm wide awake, young oysterman, and all the folks away."

Then up arose the oysterman, and to himself said he,
"I guess I 'll leave the skiff at home, for fear that folks should see;
I read it in the story-book, that, for to kiss his dear,
Leander swam the Hellespont, — and I will swim this here."

And he has leaped into the waves, and crossed the shining stream,
And he has clambered up the bank, all in the moonlight gleam;
O there were kisses sweet as dew, and words as soft as rain, —
But they have heard her father's step, and in he leaps again!

Out spoke the ancient fisherman, — "O what was that, my daughter?"
"'T was nothing but a pebble, sir, I threw into the water."
"And what is that, pray tell me, love, that paddles off so fast?"
"It 's nothing but a porpoise, sir, that 's been a swimming past."

Out spoke the ancient fisherman, — "Now bring me my harpoon!
I 'll get into my fishing-boat, and fix the fellow soon."
Down fell that pretty innocent, as falls a snow-white lamb,
Her hair drooped round her pallid cheeks, like seaweed on a clam.

Alas for those two loving ones! she waked not from her swound,
And he was taken with the cramp, and in the waves was drowned;
But Fate has metamorphosed them, in pity of their woe,
And now they keep an oyster-shop for mermaids down below.

TO AN INSECT.

I LOVE to hear thine earnest voice,
Wherever thou art hid,
Thou testy little dogmatist,
Thou pretty Katydid!
Thou mindest me of gentlefolks,—
Old gentlefolks are they, —
Thou say'st an undisputed thing
In such a solemn way.

Thou art a female, Katydid!
I know it by the trill
That quivers through thy piercing notes,
So petulant and shrill.
I think there is a knot of you
Beneath the hollow tree, —
A knot of spinster Katydids, —
Do Katydids drink tea?

O tell me where did Katy live,
And what did Katy do?
And was she very fair and young,
And yet so wicked, too?
Did Katy love a naughty man,
Or kiss more cheeks than one?
I warrant Katy did no more
Than many a Kate has done.

Dear me! I 'll tell you all about
My fuss with little Jane,

And Ann, with whom I used to walk
So often down the lane,
And all that tore their locks of black,
Or wet their eyes of blue, —
Pray tell me, sweetest Katydid,
What did poor Katy do?

Ah no! the living oak shall crash,
That stood for ages still,
The rock shall rend its mossy base
And thunder down the hill,
Before the little Katydid
Shall add one word, to tell
The mystic story of the maid
Whose name she knows so well.

Peace to the ever-murmuring race!
And when the latest one
Shall fold in death her feeble wings
Beneath the autumn sun,
Then shall she raise her fainting voice,
And lift her drooping lid,
And then the child of future years
Shall hear what Katy did.

THE DILEMMA.

NOW, by the blessed Paphian queen,
Who heaves the breast of sweet sixteen;
By every name I cut on bark
Before my morning star grew dark;
By Hymen's torch, by Cupid's dart,
By all that thrills the beating heart;
The bright black eye, the melting blue, —
I cannot choose between the two.

I had a vision in my dreams; —
I saw a row of twenty beams;
From every beam a rope was hung,
In every rope a lover swung;
I asked the hue of every eye,
That bade each luckless lover die;
Ten shadowy lips said, heavenly blue,
And ten accused the darker hue.

I asked a matron which she deemed
With fairest light of beauty beamed;
She answered, some thought both were fair, —
Give her blue eyes and golden hair.
I might have liked her judgment well,
But, as she spoke, she rung the bell,
And all her girls, nor small nor few,
Came marching in, — their eyes were blue.

I asked a maiden; back she flung
The locks that round her forehead hung,

And turned her eye, a glorious one,
Bright as a diamond in the sun,
On me, until beneath its rays
I felt as if my hair would blaze;
She liked all eyes but eyes of green;
She looked at me; what could she mean?

Ah! many lids Love lurks between
Nor heeds the coloring of his screen;
And when his random arrows fly,
The victim falls, but knows not why.
Gaze not upon his shield of jet,
The shaft upon the string is set;
Look not beneath his azure veil,
Though every limb were cased in mail.

Well, both might make a martyr break
The chain that bound him to the stake;
And both, with but a single ray,
Can melt our very hearts away;
And both, when balanced, hardly seem
To stir the scales, or rock the beam;
But that is dearest, all the while,
That wears for us the sweetest smile.

DAILY TRIALS.

BY A SENSITIVE MAN.

O THERE are times
When all this fret and tumult that we hear
Do seem more stale than to the sexton's ear
His own dull chimes.

Ding dong! ding dong!
The world is in a simmer like a sea
Over a pent volcano, — woe is me
All the day long!

From crib to shroud!
Nurse o'er our cradles screameth lullaby,
And friends in boots tramp round us as we die,
Snuffling aloud.

At morning's call
The small-voiced pug-dog welcomes in the sun,
And flea-bit mongrels, wakening one by one,
Give answer all.

When evening dim
Draws round us, then the lonely caterwaul,
Tart solo, sour duet, and general squall, —
These are our hymn.

Women, with tongues
Like polar needles, ever on the jar, —
Men, plugless word-spouts, whose deep fountains are
Within their lungs.

Children, with drums
Strapped round them by the fond paternal ass,
Peripatetics with a blade of grass
Between their thumbs.

Vagrants, whose arts
Have caged some devil in their mad machine,
Which grinding, squeaks, with husky groans between,
Come out by starts.

Cockneys that kill
Thin horses of a Sunday, — men, with clams,
Hoarse as young bisons roaring for their dams
From hill to hill.

Soldiers, with guns,
Making a nuisance of the blessed air,
Child-crying bellmen, children in despair,
Screeching for buns.

Storms, thunders, waves!
Howl, crash, and bellow till ye get your fill;
Ye sometimes rest; men never can be still
But in their graves.

TO THE PORTRAIT OF "A LADY."

IN THE ATHENÆUM GALLERY.

WELL, Miss, I wonder where you live,
I wonder what 's your name,
I wonder how you came to be
In such a stylish frame;
Perhaps you were a favorite child,
Perhaps an only one;
Perhaps your friends were not aware
You had your portrait done!

Yet you must be a harmless soul;
I cannot think that Sin
Would care to throw his loaded dice,
With such a stake to win;
I cannot think you would provoke
The poet's wicked pen,
Or make young women bite their lips,
Or ruin fine young men.

Pray, did you ever hear, my love,
Of boys that go about,
Who, for a very trifling sum,
Will snip one's picture out?
I 'm not averse to red and white,
But all things have their place,
I think a profile cut in black
Would suit your style of face?

I love sweet features; I will own
That I should like myself
To see my portrait on a wall,
Or bust upon a shelf;
But nature sometimes makes one up
Of such sad odds and ends,
It really might be quite as well
Hushed up among one's friends!

REFLECTIONS OF A PROUD PEDESTRIAN.

I SAW the curl of his waving lash,
And the glance of his knowing eye,
And I knew that he thought he was cutting a dash,
As his steed went thundering by.

And he may ride in the rattling gig,
Or flourish the Stanhope gay,
And dream that he looks exceeding big
To the people that walk in the way;

But he shall think, when the night is still,
On the stable-boy's gathering numbers,
And the ghost of many a veteran bill
Shall hover around his slumbers;

The ghastly dun shall worry his sleep,
And constables cluster around him,
And he shall creep from the wood-hole deep
Where their spectre eyes have found him!

Ay! gather your reins, and crack your thong,
    And bid your steed go faster;
He does not know, as he scrambles along,
    That he has a fool for his master;

And hurry away on your lonely ride,
    Nor deign from the mire to save me;
I will paddle it stoutly at your side
    With the tandem that nature gave me!

THE DORCHESTER GIANT.

THERE was a giant in time of old,
A mighty one was he;
He had a wife, but she was a scold,
So he kept her shut in his mammoth fold;
And he had children three.

It happened to be an election day,
And the giants were choosing a king;
The people were not democrats then,
They did not talk of the rights of men,
And all that sort of thing.

Then the giant took his children three,
And fastened them in the pen;
The children roared; quoth the giant, "Be still!"
And Dorchester Heights and Milton Hill
Rolled back the sound again.

Then he brought them a pudding stuffed with plums,
As big as the State-House dome;
Quoth he, "There 's something for you to eat;
So stop your mouths with your 'lection treat,
And wait till your dad comes home."

So the giant pulled him a chestnut stout,
And whittled the boughs away;
The boys and their mother set up a shout,
Said he, "You 're in, and you can't get out,
Bellow as loud as you may."

Off he went, and he growled a tune
    As he strode the fields along;
'T is said a buffalo fainted away,
And fell as cold as a lump of clay,
    When he heard the giant's song.

But whether the story 's true or not,
    It is not for me to show;
There 's many a thing that 's twice as queer
In somebody's lectures that we hear,
    And those are true, you know.

* * * * *

What are those lone ones doing now,
    The wife and the children sad?
O, they are in a terrible rout,
Screaming, and throwing their pudding about,
    Acting as they were mad.

They flung it over to Roxbury hills,
    They flung it over the plain,
And all over Milton and Dorchester too
Great lumps of pudding the giants threw;
    They tumbled as thick as rain.

* * * * *

Giant and mammoth have passed away,
    For ages have floated by;
The suet is hard as a marrow-bone,
And every plum is turned to a stone,
    But there the puddings lie.

And if, some pleasant afternoon,
    You 'll ask me out to ride,
The whole of the story I will tell,
And you shall see where the puddings fell,
    And pay for the punch beside.

THE MUSIC-GRINDERS.

THERE are three ways in which men take
One's money from his purse,
And very hard it is to tell
Which of the three is worse;
But all of them are bad enough
To make a body curse.

You 're riding out some pleasant day,
And counting up your gains;
A fellow jumps from out a bush,
And takes your horse's reins,
Another hints some words about
A bullet in your brains.

It 's hard to meet such pressing friends
In such a lonely spot;

It 's very hard to lose your cash,
But harder to be shot;
And so you take your wallet out,
Though you would rather not.

Perhaps you 're going out to dine, —
Some filthy creature begs
You 'll hear about the cannon-ball
That carried off his pegs,
And says it is a dreadful thing
For men to lose their legs.

He tells you of his starving wife,
His children to be fed,
Poor little, lovely innocents,
All clamorous for bread, —
And so you kindly help to put
A bachelor to bed.

You 're sitting on your window-seat,
Beneath a cloudless moon;
You hear a sound, that seems to wear
The semblance of a tune,
As if a broken fife should strive
To drown a cracked bassoon.

And nearer, nearer still, the tide
Of music seems to come,
There 's something like a human voice,
And something like a drum;
You sit in speechless agony,
Until your ear is numb.

Poor "home, sweet home" should seem to be
A very dismal place;
Your "auld acquaintance" all at once
Is altered in the face;
Their discords sting through Burns and Moore,
Like hedgehogs dressed in lace.

You think they are crusaders, sent
From some infernal clime,
To pluck the eyes of Sentiment,
And dock the tail of Rhyme,
To crack the voice of Melody,
And break the legs of Time.

But hark! the air again is still,
The music all is ground,
And silence, like a poultice, comes
To heal the blows of sound;
It cannot be, — it is, — it is, —
A hat is going round!

No! Pay the dentist when he leaves
A fracture in your jaw,
And pay the owner of the bear,
That stunned you with his paw,
And buy the lobster that has had
Your knuckles in his claw;

But if you are a portly man,
Put on your fiercest frown,
And talk about a constable
To turn them out of town;
Then close your sentence with an oath,
And shut the window down!

And if you are a slender man,
    Not big enough for that,
Or, if you cannot make a speech,
    Because you are a flat,
Go very quietly and drop
    A button in the hat!

THE SEPTEMBER GALE.

I'M not a chicken; I have seen
    Full many a chill September,
And though I was a youngster then,
    That gale I well remember;
The day before, my kite-string snapped,
    And I, my kite pursuing,
The wind whisked off my palm-leaf hat; —
    For me two storms were brewing!

It came as quarrels sometimes do,
    When married folks get clashing;
There was a heavy sigh or two,
    Before the fire was flashing, —
A little stir among the clouds,
    Before they rent asunder, —
A little rocking of the trees,
    And then came on the thunder.

Lord! how the ponds and rivers boiled,
    And how the shingles rattled!

And oaks were scattered on the ground,
 As if the Titans battled;
And all above was in a howl,
 And all below a clatter, —
The earth was like a frying-pan,
 Or some such hissing matter.

It chanced to be our washing-day,
 And all our things were drying:
The storm came roaring through the lines,
 And set them all a flying;
I saw the shirts and petticoats
 Go riding off like witches;
I lost, ah! bitterly I wept, —
 I lost my Sunday breeches!

I saw them straddling through the air,
 Alas! too late to win them;
I saw them chase the clouds, as if
 The Devil had been in them;
They were my darlings and my pride,
 My boyhood's only riches, —
"Farewell, farewell," I faintly cried, —
 "My breeches! O my breeches!"

That night I saw them in my dreams,
 How changed from what I knew them!
The dews had steeped their faded threads,
 The winds had whistled through them!
I saw the wide and ghastly rents
 Where demon claws had torn them;
A hole was in their amplest part,
 As if an imp had worn them.

I have had many happy years,
And tailors kind and clever,
But those young pantaloons have gone
Forever and forever!
And not till fate has cut the last
Of all my earthly stitches,
This aching heart shall cease to mourn
My loved, my long-lost breeches!

THE TOADSTOOL.

THERE 'S a thing that grows by the fainting flower,
And springs in the shade of the lady's bower;
The lily shrinks, and the rose turns pale,
When they feel its breath in the summer gale,
And the tulip curls its leaves in pride,
And the blue-eyed violet starts aside;
But the lily may flaunt, and the tulip stare,
For what does the honest toadstool care?

She does not glow in a painted vest,
And she never blooms on the maiden's breast;
But she comes, as the saintly sisters do,
In a modest suit of a Quaker hue.
And, when the stars in the evening skies
Are weeping dew from their gentle eyes,
The toad comes out from his hermit cell,
The tale of his faithful love to tell.

O there is light in her lover's glance,
That flies to her heart like a silver lance;
His breeches are made of spotted skin,
His jacket is tight, and his pumps are thin;
In a cloudless night you may hear his song,
As its pensive melody floats along,
And, if you will look by the moonlight fair,
The trembling form of the toad is there.

And he twines his arms round her slender stem,
In the shade of her velvet diadem;
But she turns away in her maiden shame,
And will not breathe on the kindling flame;
He sings at her feet through the livelong night,
And creeps to his cave at the break of light;
And whenever he comes to the air above,
His throat his swelling with baffled love.

THE SPECTRE PIG.

A BALLAD.

IT was the stalwart butcher man,
That knit his swarthy brow,
And said the gentle Pig must die,
And sealed it with a vow.

And oh! it was the gentle Pig
Lay stretched upon the ground,
And ah! it was the cruel knife
His little heart that found.

They took him then, those wicked men,
They trailed him all along;
They put a stick between his lips,
And through his heels a thong;

And round and round an oaken beam
A hempen cord they flung,
And, like a mighty pendulum,
All solemnly he swung!

Now say thy prayers, thou sinful man,
And think what thou hast done,
And read thy catechism well,
Thou bloody-minded one;

For if his sprite should walk by night,
It better were for thee,

That thou wert mouldering in the ground,
    Or bleaching in the sea.

It was the savage butcher then,
    That made a mock of sin,
And swore a very wicked oath,
    He did not care a pin.

It was the butcher's youngest son, —
    His voice was broke with sighs,
And with his pocket-handkerchief
    He wiped his little eyes;

All young and ignorant was he,
    But innocent and mild,
And, in his soft simplicity,
    Out spoke the tender child: —

"O father, father, list to me;
    The Pig is deadly sick,
And men have hung him by his heels,
    And fed him with a stick."

It was the bloody butcher then,
    That laughed as he would die,
Yet did he soothe the sorrowing child,
    And bid him not to cry; —

"O Nathan, Nathan, what 's a Pig,
    That thou shouldst weep and wail?
Come, bear thee like a butcher's child,
    And thou shalt have his tail!"

It was the butcher's daughter then,
　　So slender and so fair,
That sobbed as if her heart would break,
　　And tore her yellow hair;

And thus she spoke in thrilling tone,—
　　Fast fell the tear-drops big;—
"Ah! woe is me! Alas! Alas!
　　The Pig! The Pig! The Pig!"

Then did her wicked father's lips
　　Make merry with her woe,
And call her many a naughty name,
　　Because she whimpered so.

Ye need not weep, ye gentle ones,
　　In vain your tears are shed,
Ye cannot wash his crimson hand,
　　Ye cannot soothe the dead.

The bright sun folded on his breast
　　His robes of rosy flame,
And softly over all the west
　　The shades of evening came.

He slept, and troops of murdered Pigs
　　Were busy with his dreams;
Loud rang their wild, unearthly shrieks,
　　Wide yawned their mortal seams.

The clock struck twelve; the Dead hath heard;
　　He opened both his eyes,
And sullenly he shook his tail
　　To lash the feeding flies.

One quiver of the hempen cord, —
    One struggle and one bound, —
With stiffened limb and leaden eye,
    The Pig was on the ground!

And straight towards the sleeper's house
    His fearful way he wended;
And hooting owl, and hovering bat,
    On midnight wing attended.

Back flew the bolt, up rose the latch,
    And open swung the door,
And little mincing feet were heard
    Pat, pat along the floor.

Two hoofs upon the sanded floor,
    And two upon the bed;
And they are breathing side by side,
    The living and the dead!

"Now wake, now wake, thou butcher man!
    What makes thy cheek so pale?
Take hold! take hold! thou dost not fear
    To clasp a spectre's tail?"

Untwisted every winding coil;
    The shuddering wretch took hold,
All like an icicle it seemed,
    So tapering and so cold.

"Thou com'st with me, thou butcher man!" —
    He strives to loose his grasp,
But, faster than the clinging vine,
    Those twining spirals clasp.

And open, open swung the door,
  And, fleeter than the wind,
The shadowy spectre swept before,
  The butcher trailed behind.

Fast fled the darkness of the night,
  And morn rose faint and dim;
They called full loud, they knocked full long,
  They did not waken him.

Straight, straight towards that oaken beam,
  A trampled pathway ran;
A ghastly shape was swinging there, —
  It was the butcher man.

THE TREADMILL SONG.

THE stars are rolling in the sky,
  The earth rolls on below,
And we can feel the rattling wheel
  Revolving as we go.
Then tread away, my gallant boys,
  And make the axle fly;
Why should not wheels go round about,
  Like planets in the sky?

Wake up, wake up, my duck-legged man,
  And stir your solid pegs!
Arouse, arouse, my gawky friend,
  And shake your spider legs;

What though you 're awkward at the trade,
There 's time enough to learn, —
So lean upon the rail, my lad,
And take another turn.

They 've built us up a noble wall,
To keep the vulgar out;
We 've nothing in the world to do,
But just to walk about;
So faster, now, you middle men,
And try to beat the ends, —
It 's pleasant work to ramble round
Among one's honest friends.

Here, tread upon the long man's toes,
He sha'n't be lazy here, —
And punch the little fellow's ribs,
And tweak that lubber's ear, —
He 's lost them both, — don't pull his hair,
Because he wears a scratch,
But poke him in the further eye,
That is n't in the patch.

Hark! fellows, there 's the supper-bell,
And so our work is done;
It 's pretty sport, — suppose we take
A round or two for fun!
If ever they should turn me out,
When I have better grown,
Now hang me, but I mean to have
A treadmill of my own!

MY AUNT.

MY aunt! my dear unmarried aunt!
Long years have o'er her flown;
Yet still she strains the aching clasp
That binds her virgin zone;
I know it hurts her, — though she looks
As cheerful as she can;
Her waist is ampler than her life,
For life is but a span.

My aunt! my poor deluded aunt!
Her hair is almost gray;

Why will she train that winter curl
In such a spring-like way?
How can she lay her glasses down,
And say she reads as well,
When, through a double convex lens,
She just makes out to spell?

Her father, — grandpapa! forgive
This erring lip its smiles —
Vowed she should make the finest girl
Within a hundred miles;
He sent her to a stylish school;
'T was in her thirteenth June;
And with her, as the rules required,
"Two towels and a spoon."

They braced my aunt against a board,
To make her straight and tall;
They laced her up, they starved her down,
To make her light and small;
They pinched her feet, they singed her hair,
They screwed it up with pins; —
O never mortal suffered more
In penance for her sins.

So, when my precious aunt was done,
My grandsire brought her back;
(By daylight, lest some rabid youth
Might follow on the track;)
"Ah!" said my grandsire, as he shook
Some powder in his pan,
"What could this lovely creature do
Against a desperate man!"

Alas! nor chariot, nor barouche,
Nor bandit cavalcade,
Tore from the trembling father's arms
His all-accomplished maid.
For her how happy had it been!
And Heaven had spared to me
To see one sad, ungathered rose
On my ancestral tree.

LINES

RECITED AT THE BERKSHIRE FESTIVAL.

COME back to your mother, ye children, for shame,
Who have wandered like truants, for riches or fame!
With a smile on her face, and a sprig in her cap,
She calls you to feast from her bountiful lap.

Come out from your alleys, your courts, and your lanes,
And breathe, like young eagles, the air of our plains;
Take a whiff from our fields, and your excellent wives
Will declare it 's all nonsense insuring your lives.

Come you of the law, who can talk, if you please,
Till the man of the moon will allow it 's a cheese,
And leave "the old lady, that never tells lies,"
To sleep with her handkerchief over her eyes.

Ye healers of men, for a moment decline
Your feats in the rhubarb and ipecac line;

While you shut up your turnpike, your neighbors can go,
The old roundabout road, to the regions below.

You clerk, on whose ears are a couple of pens,
And whose head is an ant-hill of units and tens;
Though Plato denies you, we welcome you still
As a featherless biped, in spite of your quill.

Poor drudge of the city! how happy he feels,
With the burs on his legs, and the grass at his heels!
No *dodger* behind, his bandannas to share,
No constable grumbling, "You must n't walk there!"

In yonder green meadow, to memory dear,
He slaps a mosquito and brushes a tear;
The dew-drops hang round him on blossoms and shoots,
He breathes but one sigh for his youth and his boots.

There stands the old school-house, hard by the old church;
That tree at its side had the flavor of birch;
O sweet were the days of his juvenile tricks,
Though the prairie of youth had so many "big licks."

By the side of yon river he weeps and he slumps,
The boots fill with water, as if they were pumps,
Till, sated with rapture, he steals to his bed,
With a glow in his heart and a cold in his head.

'T is past, — he is dreaming, — I see him again;
The ledger returns as by legerdemain;
His neckcloth is damp with an easterly flaw,
And he holds in his fingers an omnibus straw.

He dreams the chill gust is a blossomy gale,
That the straw is a rose from his dear native vale;
And murmurs, unconscious of space and of time,
"A 1. Extra-super. Ah, is n't it PRIME!"

O what are the prizes we perish to win
To the first little "shiner" we caught with a pin!
No soil upon earth is so dear to our eyes
As the soil we first stirred in terrestrial pies!

Then come from all parties, and parts, to our feast;
Though not at the "Astor," we 'll give you at least
A bite at an apple, a seat on the grass,
And the best of old — water — at nothing a glass.

VERSES FOR AFTER-DINNER.

Φ Β Κ SOCIETY, 1844.

I WAS thinking last night, as I sat in the cars,
With the charmingest prospect of cinders and stars,
Next Thursday is — bless me! — how hard it will be,
If that cannibal president calls upon me!

There is nothing on earth that he will not devour,
From a tutor in seed to a freshman in flower;
No sage is too gray, and no youth is too green,
And you can't be too plump, though you 're never too lean.

While others enlarge on the boiled and the roast,
He serves a raw clergyman up with a toast,
Or catches some doctor, quite tender and young,
And basely insists on a bit of his tongue.

Poor victim, prepared for his classical spit,
With a stuffing of praise, and a basting of wit,
You may twitch at your collar, and wrinkle your brow,
But you 're up on your legs, and you 're in for it now.

O think of your friends, — they are waiting to hear
Those jokes that are thought so remarkably queer;
And all the Jack Horners of metrical buns
Are prying and fingering to pick out the puns.

Those thoughts which, like chickens, will always thrive best
When reared by the heat of the natural nest,
Will perish if hatched from their embryo dream
In the mist and the glow of convivial steam.

O pardon me, then, if I meekly retire,
With a very small flash of ethereal fire;
No rubbing will kindle your Lucifer match,
If the *fiz* does not follow the primitive scratch.

Dear friends, who are listening so sweetly the while,
With your lips double reefed in a snug little smile, —
I leave you two fables, both drawn from the deep, —
The shells you can drop, but the pearls you may keep.

* * * * *

The fish called the FLOUNDER, perhaps you may know,
Has one side for use and another for show;
One side for the public, a delicate brown,
And one that is white, which he always keeps down.

A very young flounder, the flattest of flats,
(And they 're none of them thicker than opera hats,)
Was speaking more freely than charity taught
Of a friend and relation that just had been caught.

"My! what an exposure! just see what a sight!
I blush for my race, — he is showing his white!
Such spinning and wriggling, — why, what does he wish?
How painfully small to respectable fish!"

Then said an old SCULPIN, — "My freedom excuse,
But you 're playing the cobbler with holes in your shoes;
Your brown side is up, — but just wait till you 're tried
And you 'll find that all flounders are white on one side."

* * * * *

There 's a slice near the PICKEREL'S pectoral fins,
Where the *thorax* leaves off and the *venter* begins;
Which his brother, survivor of fish-hooks and lines,
Though fond of his family, never declines.

He loves his relations; he feels they 'll be missed;
But that one little titbit he cannot resist;
So your bait may be swallowed, no matter how fast,
For you catch your next fish with a piece of the last.

And thus, O survivor, whose merciless fate
Is to take the next hook with the president's bait,
You are lost while you snatch from the end of his line
The morsel he rent from this bosom of mine!

A SONG

FOR THE CENTENNIAL CELEBRATION OF HARVARD COLLEGE, 1836.

WHEN the Puritans came over,
Our hills and swamps to clear,
The woods were full of catamounts,
And Indians red as deer,
With tomahawks and scalping-knives,
That make folks' heads look queer ; —
O the ship from England used to bring
A hundred wigs a year !

The crows came cawing through the air
To pluck the pilgrims' corn,
The bears came snuffing round the door
Whene'er a babe was born,
The rattlesnakes were bigger round
Than the but of the old ram's horn
The deacon blew at meeting time
On every "Sabbath" morn.

But soon they knocked the wigwams down,
And pine-tree trunk and limb
Began to sprout among the leaves
In shape of steeples slim ;
And out the little wharves were stretched
Along the ocean's rim,
And up the little school-house shot
To keep the boys in trim.

And, when at length the College rose,
The sachem cocked his eye
At every tutor's meagre ribs
Whose coat-tails whistled by :
But when the Greek and Hebrew words
Came tumbling from their jaws,
The copper-colored children all
Ran screaming to the squaws.

And who was on the Catalogue
When college was begun ?
Two nephews of the President,
And *the* Professor's son ;
(They turned a little Indian by,
As brown as any bun ;)
Lord ! how the seniors knocked about
The freshman class of one !

They had not then the dainty things
That commons now afford,
But *succotash* and *homony*
Were smoking on the board ;
They did not rattle round in gigs,
Or dash in long-tail blues,
But always on Commencement days
The tutors blacked their shoes.

God bless the ancient Puritans !
Their lot was hard enough ;
But honest hearts make iron arms,
And tender maids are tough ;
So love and faith have formed and fed
Our true-born Yankee stuff,
And keep the kernel in the shell
The British found so rough !

EVENING.

BY A TAILOR.

DAY hath put on his jacket, and around
His burning bosom buttoned it with stars.
Here will I lay me on the velvet grass,
That is like padding to earth's meagre ribs,
And hold communion with the things about me.
Ah me! how lovely is the golden braid
That binds the skirt of night's descending robe!
The thin leaves, quivering on their silken threads,
Do make a music like to rustling satin,
As the light breezes smooth their downy nap.

Ha! what is this that rises to my touch,
So like a cushion? Can it be a cabbage?
It is, it is that deeply injured flower,
Which boys do flout us with; — but yet I love thee,
Thou giant rose, wrapped in a green surtout.
Doubtless in Eden thou didst blush as bright

As these, thy puny brethren ; and thy breath
Sweetened the fragrance of her spicy air ;
But now thou seemest like a bankrupt beau,
Stripped of his gaudy hues and essences,
And growing portly in his sober garments.

Is that a swan that rides upon the water ?
O no, it is that other gentle bird,
Which is the patron of our noble calling.
I well remember, in my early years,
When these young hands first closed upon a goose ;
I have a scar upon my thimble finger,
Which chronicles the hour of young ambition.
My father was a tailor, and his father,
And my sire's grandsire, all of them were tailors ;
They had an ancient goose, — it was an heir-loom
From some remoter tailor of our race.
It happened I did see it on a time
When none was near, and I did deal with it,
And it did burn me, — oh, most fearfully !

It is a joy to straighten out one's limbs,
And leap elastic from the level counter,
Leaving the petty grievances of earth,
The breaking thread, the din of clashing shears,
And all the needles that do wound the spirit,
For such a pensive hour of soothing silence.
Kind Nature, shuffling in her loose undress,
Lays bare her shady bosom ; — I can feel
With all around me ; — I can hail the flowers
That sprig earth's mantle, — and yon quiet bird,
That rides the stream, is to me as a brother.
The vulgar know not all the hidden pockets,

Where Nature stows away her loveliness.
But this unnatural posture of the legs
Cramps my extended calves, and I must go
Where I can coil them in their wonted fashion.

NUX POSTCŒNATICA.

I WAS sitting with my microscope, upon my parlor rug,
With a very heavy quarto and a very lively bug;
The true bug had been organized with only two antennæ,
But the humbug in the copper-plate would have them twice as many.

And I thought, like Dr. Faustus, of the emptiness of art,
How we take a fragment for the whole, and call the whole a part,
When I heard a heavy footstep that was loud enough for two,
And a man of forty entered, exclaiming, — "How d' ye do?"

He was not a ghost, my visitor, but solid flesh and bone;
He wore a Palo Alto hat, his weight was twenty stone;
(It 's odd how hats expand their brims as riper years invade,
As if when life had reached its noon, it wanted them for shade!)

I lost my focus, — dropped my book, — the bug, who was a flea,
At once exploded, and commenced experiments on me.
They have a certain heartiness that frequently appalls, —
Those mediæval gentlemen in semilunar smalls!

"My boy," he said, — (colloquial ways, — the vast, broad-hatted man,) —
"Come dine with us on Thursday next, — you must, you know you can;

We 're going to have a roaring time, with lots of fun and noise,
Distinguished guests, et cetera, the JUDGE, and all the boys."

Not so, — I said, — my temporal bones are showing pretty clear
It 's time to stop, — just look and see that hair above this ear;
My golden days are more than spent, — and, what is very strange,
If these are real silver hairs, I 'm getting lots of change.

Besides — my prospects — don't you know that people won't employ
A man that wrongs his manliness by laughing like a boy?
And suspect the azure blossom that unfolds upon a shoot,
As if wisdom's old potato could not flourish at its root?

It 's a very fine reflection, when you 're etching out a smile
On a copper-plate of faces that would stretch at least a mile,
That, what with sneers from enemies, and cheapening shrugs of friends,
It will cost you all the earnings that a month of labor lends!

It 's a vastly pleasing prospect, when you 're screwing out a laugh,
That your very next year's income is diminished by a half,
And a little boy trips barefoot that Pegasus may go,
And the baby's milk is watered that your Helicon may flow!

No; — the joke has been a good one, — but I 'm getting fond of quiet,
And I don't like deviations from my customary diet;
So I think I will not go with you to hear the toasts and speeches,
But stick to old Montgomery Place, and have some pig and peaches.

The fat man answered: — Shut your mouth, and hear the genuine creed;
The true essentials of a feast are only fun and feed;

The force that wheels the planets round delights in spinning tops,
And that young earthquake t' other day was great at shaking props.

I tell you what, philosopher, if all the longest heads
That ever knocked their sinciputs in stretching on their beds
Were round one great mahogany, I 'd beat those fine old folks
With twenty dishes, twenty fools, and twenty clever jokes!

Why, if Columbus should be there, the company would beg
He 'd show that little trick of his of balancing the egg!
Milton to Stilton would give in, and Solomon to Salmon,
And Roger Bacon be a bore, and Francis Bacon gammon!

And as for all the "patronage" of all the clowns and boors
That squint their little narrow eyes at any freak of yours,
Do leave them to your prosier friends, — such fellows ought to die
When rhubarb is so very scarce and ipecac so high!

And so I come, — like Lochinvar, to tread a single measure,
To purchase with a loaf of bread a sugar-plum of pleasure,
To enter for the cup of glass that 's run for after dinner,
Which yields a single sparkling draught, then breaks and cuts the winner.

Ah, that 's the way delusion comes, — a glass of old Madeira,
A pair of visual diaphragms revolved by Jane or Sarah,
And down go vows and promises without the slightest question
If eating words won't compromise the organs of digestion!

And yet, among my native shades, beside my nursing mother,
Where every stranger seems a friend, and every friend a brother,
I feel the old convivial glow (unaided) o'er me stealing, —
The warm, champagny, old-particular, brandy-punchy feeling.

We 're all alike; — Vesuvius flings the scoriæ from his fountain,
But down they come in volleying rain back to the burning mountain;
We leave, like those volcanic stones, our precious Alma Mater,
But will keep dropping in again to see the dear old crater.

THE STETHOSCOPE SONG.

A PROFESSIONAL BALLAD.

THERE was a young man in Boston town,
He bought him a STETHOSCOPE nice and new,
All mounted and finished and polished down,
With an ivory cap and a stopper too.

It happened a spider within did crawl,
And spun a web of ample size,
Wherein there chanced one day to fall
A couple of very imprudent flies.

The first was a bottle-fly, big and blue,
The second was smaller, and thin and long;
So there was a concert between the two,
Like an octave flute and a tavern gong.

Now being from Paris but recently,
This fine young man would show his skill;
And so they gave him, his hand to try,
A hospital patient extremely ill.

Some said that his *liver* was short of *bile*,
And some that his *heart* was over size,
While some kept arguing all the while
He was crammed with *tubercles* up to his eyes.

This fine young man then up stepped he,
And all the doctors made a pause;
Said he, — The man must die, you see,
By the fifty-seventh of Louis's laws.

But since the case is a desperate one,
To explore his chest it may be well;
For if he should die and it were not done,
You know the *autopsy* would not tell.

Then out his stethoscope he took,
And on it placed his curious ear;
Mon Dieu! said he, with a knowing look,
Why here is a sound that 's mighty queer!

The *bourdonnement* is very clear, —
Amphoric buzzing, as I 'm alive!
Five doctors took their turn to hear;
Amphoric buzzing, said all the five.

There 's *empyema* beyond a doubt;
We 'll plunge a *trocar* in his side. —
The diagnosis was made out,
They tapped the patient; so he died.

Now such as hate new-fashioned toys
Began to look extremely glum;
They said that *rattles* were made for boys,
And vowed that his *buzzing* was all a hum.

There was an old lady had long been sick,
    And what was the matter none did know:
Her pulse was slow, though her tongue was quick;
    To her this knowing youth must go.

So there the nice old lady sat,
    With phials and boxes all in a row;
She asked the young doctor what he was at,
    To thump her and tumble her ruffles so.

Now, when the stethoscope came out,
    The flies began to buzz and whiz; —
O ho! the matter is clear, no doubt;
    An *aneurism* there plainly is.

The *bruit de râpe* and the *bruit de scie*
    And the *bruit de diable* are all combined;
How happy Bouillaud would be,
    If he a case like this could find!

Now, when the neighboring doctors found
    A case so rare had been descried,
They every day her ribs did pound
    In squads of twenty; so she died.

Then six young damsels, slight and frail,
    Received this kind young doctor's cares;
They all were getting slim and pale,
    And short of breath on mounting stairs.

They all made rhymes with "sighs" and "skies,"
    And loathed their puddings and buttered rolls,
And dieted, much to their friends' surprise,
    On pickles and pencils and chalk and coals.

So fast their little hearts did bound,
The frightened insects buzzed the more;
So over all their chests he found
The *râle sifflant*, and *râle sonore*.

He shook his head; — there 's grave disease, —
I greatly fear you all must die;
A slight *post-mortem*, if you please,
Surviving friends would gratify.

The six young damsels wept aloud,
Which so prevailed on six young men,
That each his honest love avowed,
Whereat they all got well again.

This poor young man was all aghast;
The price of stethoscopes came down;
And so he was reduced at last
To practise in a country town.

The doctors being very sore,
A stethoscope they did devise,
That had a rammer to clear the bore,
With a knob at the end to kill the flies.

Now use your ears, all you that can,
But don't forget to mind your eyes,
Or you may be cheated, like this young man
By a couple of silly, abnormal flies.

ON LENDING A PUNCH-BOWL.

THIS ancient silver bowl of mine, — it tells of good old times,
Of joyous days, and jolly nights, and merry Christmas chimes;
They were a free and jovial race, but honest, brave, and true,
That dipped their ladle in the punch when this old bowl was new.

A Spanish galleon brought the bar, — so runs the ancient tale;
'T was hammered by an Antwerp smith, whose arm was like a
flail;
And now and then between the strokes, for fear his strength
should fail,
He wiped his brow, and quaffed a cup of good old Flemish ale.

'T was purchased by an English squire to please his loving dame,
Who saw the cherubs, and conceived a longing for the same;
And oft as on the ancient stock another twig was found,
'T was filled with caudle spiced and hot, and handed smoking
round.

But, changing hands, it reached at length a Puritan divine,
Who used to follow Timothy, and take a little wine,
But hated punch and prelacy; and so it was, perhaps,
He went to Leyden, where he found conventicles and schnaps.

And then, of course, you know what 's next, — it left the Dutchman's shore
With those that in the Mayflower came, — a hundred souls and
more, —
Along with all the furniture, to fill their new abodes, —
To judge by what is still on hand, at least a hundred loads.

'T was on a dreary winter's eve, the night was closing dim,
When old Miles Standish took the bowl, and filled it to the brim;
The little Captain stood and stirred the posset with his sword,
And all his sturdy men-at-arms were ranged about the board.

He poured the fiery Hollands in, — the man that never feared, —
He took a long and solemn draught, and wiped his yellow beard;
And one by one the musketeers — the men that fought and
prayed —
All drank as 't were their mother's milk, and not a man afraid.

That night, affrighted from his nest, the screaming eagle flew,
He heard the Pequot's ringing whoop, the soldier's wild halloo;
And there the sachem learned the rule he taught to kith and kin,
"Run from the white man when you find he smells of Hollands
gin!"

A hundred years, and fifty more, had spread their leaves and snows,
A thousand rubs had flattened down each little cherub's nose,
When once again the bowl was filled, but not in mirth or joy,
'T was mingled by a mother's hand to cheer her parting boy.

Drink, John, she said, 't will do you good, — poor child, you 'll never bear
This working in the dismal trench, out in the midnight air;
And if — God bless me! — you were hurt, 't would keep away the chill;
So John *did* drink, — and well he wrought that night at Bunker's Hill!

I tell you, there was generous warmth in good old English cheer;
I tell you, 't was a pleasant thought to bring its symbol here.
'T is but the fool that loves excess; — hast thou a drunken soul?
Thy bane is in thy shallow skull, not in my silver bowl!

I love the memory of the past, — its pressed yet fragrant flowers, —
The moss that clothes its broken walls, — the ivy on its towers; —
Nay, this poor bauble it bequeathed, — my eyes grow moist and dim,
To think of all the vanished joys that danced around its brim.

Then fill a fair and honest cup, and bear it straight to me;
The goblet hallows all it holds, whate'er the liquid be;
And may the cherubs on its face protect me from the sin,
That dooms one to those dreadful words, — "My dear, where *have* you been?"

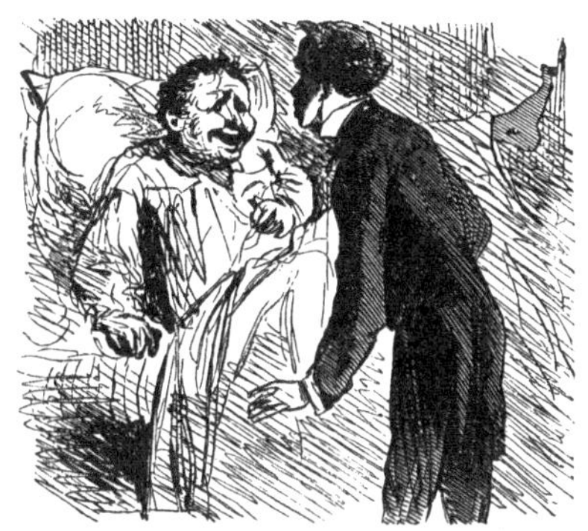

THE HEIGHT OF THE RIDICULOUS.

I WROTE some lines once on a time
In wondrous merry mood,
And thought, as usual, men would say
They were exceeding good.

They were so queer, so very queer,
I laughed as I would die;
Albeit, in the general way,
A sober man am I.

I called my servant, and he came;
How kind it was of him,
To mind a slender man like me,
He of the mighty limb!

"These to the printer," I exclaimed,
And, in my humorous way,

I added, (as a trifling jest,)
"There 'll be the devil to pay."

He took the paper, and I watched,
And saw him peep within;
At the first line he read, his face
Was all upon the grin.

He read the next; the grin grew broad,
And shot from ear to ear;
He read the third; a chuckling noise
I now began to hear.

The fourth; he broke into a roar;
The fifth; his waistband split;
The sixth; he burst five buttons off,
And tumbled in a fit.

Ten days and nights, with sleepless eye,
I watched that wretched man,
And since, I never dare to write
As funny as I can.

LATTER-DAY WARNINGS.

WHEN legislators keep the law,
When banks dispense with bolts and locks, —
When berries — whortle, rasp, and straw —
Grow bigger *downwards* through the box, —

When he that selleth house or land
  Shows leak in roof or flaw in right, —
When haberdashers choose the stand
  Whose window hath the broadest light, —

When preachers tell us all they think,
  And party leaders all they mean, —
When what we pay for, that we drink,
  From real grape and coffee-bean, —

When lawyers take what they would give,
  And doctors give what they would take, —
When city fathers eat to live,
  Save when they fast for conscience' sake, —

When one that hath a horse on sale
  Shall bring his merit to the proof,
Without a lie for every nail
  That holds the iron on the hoof, —

When in the usual place for rips
  Our gloves are stitched with special care,
And guarded well the whalebone tips
  Where first umbrellas need repair, —

When Cuba's weeds have quite forgot
  The power of suction to resist,
And claret-bottles harbor not
  Such dimples as would hold your fist, —

When publishers no longer steal,
  And pay for what they stole before, —
When the first locomotive's wheel
  Rolls through the Hoosac tunnel's bore; —

Till then let Cumming blaze away,
  And Miller's saints blow up the globe;
But when you see that blessed day,
  Then order your ascension robe!

PROLOGUE.

A PROLOGUE? Well, of course the ladies know; —
I have my doubts. No matter, — here we go!
What is a Prologue? Let our Tutor teach:
Pro means beforehand; *logos* stands for speech.
'T is like the harper's prelude on the strings,
The primá donna's courtesy ere she sings: —
Prologues in metre are to other *pros*
As worsted stockings are to engine-hose.

"The world 's a stage," — as Shakespeare said, one day;
The stage a world — was what he meant to say.
The outside world 's a blunder, that is clear;
The real world that Nature meant is here.
Here every foundling finds its lost mamma;
Each rogue, repentant, melts his stern papa;
Misers relent, the spendthrift's debts are paid,
The cheats are taken in the traps they laid;
One after one the troubles all are past
Till the fifth act comes right side up at last,
When the young couple, old folks, rogues, and all,
Join hands, *so* happy at the curtain's fall.
Here suffering virtue ever finds relief,
And black-browed ruffians always come to grief.

When the lorn damsel, with a frantic screech,
And cheeks as hueless as a brandy-peach,
Cries, "Help, kyind Heaven!" and drops upon her knees
On the green — baize, — beneath the (canvas) trees, —
See to her side avenging Valor fly: —
"Ha! Villain! Draw! Now, Terraitorr, yield or die!"
When the poor hero flounders in despair,
Some dear lost uncle turns up millionnaire,
Clasps the young scapegrace with paternal joy,
Sobs on his neck, "*My boy!* MY BOY!! MY BOY!!!"

Ours, then, sweet friends, the real world to-night,
Of love that conquers in disaster's spite.
Ladies, attend! While woful cares and doubt
Wrong the soft passion in the world without,
Though fortune scowl, though prudence interfere,
One thing is certain: Love will triumph here!
Lords of creation, whom your ladies rule, —
The world's great masters, when you 're out of school, —
Learn the brief moral of our evening's play:
Man has his will, — but woman has her way!
While man's dull spirit toils in smoke and fire,
Woman's swift instinct threads the electric wire, —
The magic bracelet stretched beneath the waves
Beats the black giant with his score of slaves.
All earthly powers confess your sovereign art
But that one rebel, — woman's wilful heart.
All foes you master; but a woman's wit
Lets daylight through you ere you know you 're hit.
So, just to picture what her art can do,
Hear an old story, made as good as new.

Rudolph, professor of the headsman's trade,
Alike was famous for his arm and blade.

One day a prisoner Justice had to kill
Knelt at the block to test the artist's skill.
Bare-armed, swart-visaged, gaunt, and shaggy-browed,
Rudolph the headsman rose above the crowd.
His falchion lightened with a sudden gleam,
As the pike's armor flashes in the stream.
He sheathed his blade; he turned as if to go;
The victim knelt, still waiting for the blow.
"Why strikest not? Perform thy murderous act,"
The prisoner said. (His voice was slightly cracked.)
"Friend, I *have* struck," the artist straight replied;
"Wait but one moment, and yourself decide."
He held his snuff-box, — "Now then, if you please!"
The prisoner sniffed, and, with a crashing sneeze,
Off his head tumbled, — bowled along the floor, —
Bounced down the steps; — the prisoner said no more!

Woman! thy falchion is a glittering eye;
If death lurk in it, O how sweet to die!
Thou takest hearts as Rudolph took the head;
We die with love, and never dream we 're dead!

THE DEACON'S MASTERPIECE:

OR, THE WONDERFUL "ONE-HOSS SHAY."

A LOGICAL STORY.

HAVE you heard of the wonderful one-hoss shay,
That was built in such a logical way
It ran a hundred years to a day,
And then, of a sudden, it —— ah, but stay,
I 'll tell you what happened without delay,
Scaring the parson into fits,
Frightening people out of their wits, —
Have you ever heard of that, I say?

Seventeen hundred and fifty-five.
Georgius Secundus was then alive, —
Snuffy old drone from the German hive.
That was the year when Lisbon-town
Saw the earth open and gulp her down,
And Braddock's army was done so brown,
Left without a scalp to its crown.
It was on the terrible Earthquake-day
That the Deacon finished the one-hoss shay.

Now in building of chaises, I tell you what,
There is always *somewhere* a weakest spot, —
In hub, tire, felloe, in spring or thill,
In panel, or crossbar, or floor, or sill,
In screw, bolt, thoroughbrace, — lurking still,
Find it somewhere you must and will, —
Above or below, or within or without, —
And that 's the reason, beyond a doubt,
A chaise *breaks down*, but does n't *wear out*.

But the Deacon swore, (as Deacons do,
With an "I dew vum," or an "I tell *yeou*,")
He would build one shay to beat the taown
'n' the keounty 'n' all the kentry raoun';
It should be so built that it *couldn'* break daown:
— "Fur," said the Deacon, "'t 's mighty plain
Thut the weakes' place mus' stan' the strain;
'n' the way t' fix it, uz I maintain,
Is only jest
T' make that place uz strong uz the rest."

So the Deacon inquired of the village folk
Where he could find the strongest oak,
That could n't be split nor bent nor broke, —
That was for spokes and floor and sills;
He sent for lancewood to make the thills;
The crossbars were ash, from the straightest trees;
The panels of white-wood, that cuts like cheese,
But lasts like iron for things like these;
The hubs of logs from the "Settler's ellum," —
Last of its timber, — they could n't sell 'em,
Never an axe had seen their chips,
And the wedges flew from between their lips,
Their blunt ends frizzled like celery-tips;
Step and prop-iron, bolt and screw,
Spring, tire, axle, and linchpin too,
Steel of the finest, bright and blue;
Thoroughbrace bison-skin, thick and wide;
Boot, top, dasher, from tough old hide
Found in the pit when the tanner died.
That was the way he "put her through." —
"There!" said the Deacon, "naow she 'll dew!"

Do! I tell you, I rather guess
She was a wonder, and nothing less!

Colts grew horses, beards turned gray,
Deacon and deaconess dropped away,
Children and grandchildren — where were they ?
But there stood the stout old one-hoss shay
As fresh as on Lisbon-earthquake-day !

EIGHTEEN HUNDRED ; — it came and found
The Deacon's masterpiece strong and sound.
Eighteen hundred increased by ten ; —
" Hahnsum kerridge " they called it then.
Eighteen hundred and twenty came ; —
Running as usual ; much the same.
Thirty and forty at last arrive,
And then come fifty, and FIFTY-FIVE.

Little of all we value here
Wakes on the morn of its hundredth year
Without both feeling and looking queer.
In fact, there 's nothing that keeps its youth,
So far as I know, but a tree and truth.
(This is a moral that runs at large ;
Take it. — You 're welcome. — No extra charge.)

FIRST OF NOVEMBER, — the Earthquake-day. —
There are traces of age in the one-hoss shay,
A general flavor of mild decay,
But nothing local as one may say.
There could n't be, — for the Deacon's art
Had made it so like in every part
That there was n't a chance for one to start.
For the wheels were just as strong as the thills,
And the floor was just as strong as the sills,
And the panels just as strong as the floor,
And the whippletree neither less nor more,

And the back-crossbar as strong as the fore,
And spring and axle and hub *encore*.
And yet, *as a whole*, it is past a doubt
In another hour it will be *worn out!*

First of November, 'Fifty-five!
This morning the parson takes a drive.
Now, small boys, get out of the way!
Here comes the wonderful one-hoss shay,
Drawn by a rat-tailed, ewe-necked bay.
"Huddup!" said the parson. — Off went they.

The parson was working his Sunday's text, —
Had got to *fifthly*, and stopped perplexed
At what the — Moses — was coming next.
All at once the horse stood still,
Close by the meet'n'-house on the hill.
— First a shiver, and then a thrill,
Then something decidedly like a spill, —
And the parson was sitting upon a rock,
At half past nine by the meet'n'-house clock, —
Just the hour of the Earthquake shock!
— What do you think the parson found,
When he got up and stared around?
The poor old chaise in a heap or mound,
As if it had been to the mill and ground!
You see, of course, if you 're not a dunce,
How it went to pieces all at once, —
All at once, and nothing first, —
Just as bubbles do when they burst.

End of the wonderful one-hoss shay.
Logic is logic. That 's all I say.

THE OLD MAN OF THE SEA.

A NIGHTMARE DREAM BY DAYLIGHT.

DO you know the Old Man of the Sea, of the Sea?
  Have you met with that dreadful old man?
If you have n't been caught, you will be, you will be;
  For catch you he must and he can.

He does n't hold on by your throat, by your throat,
  As of old in the terrible tale;
But he grapples you tight by the coat, by the coat,
  Till its buttons and button-holes fail.

There 's the charm of a snake in his eye, in his eye,
  And a polypus-grip in his hands;
You cannot go back, nor get by, nor get by,
  If you look at the spot where he stands.

O, you 're grabbed! See his claw on your sleeve, on your sleeve!
  It is Sinbad's Old Man of the Sea!
You 're a Christian, no doubt you believe, you believe:
  You 're a martyr, whatever you be!

— Is the breakfast-hour past? They must wait, they must wait,
  While the coffee boils sullenly down,
While the Johnny-cake burns on the grate, on the grate,
  And the toast is done frightfully brown.

— Yes, your dinner will keep; let it cool, let it cool,
  And Madam may worry and fret,
And children half-starved go to school, go to school;
  He can't think of sparing you yet.

— Hark! the bell for the train! "Come along! Come along!
  For there is n't a second to lose."
"ALL ABOARD!" (He holds on.) "Fsht! ding-dong! Fsht! ding-dong!" —
  You can follow on foot, if you choose.

— There 's a maid with a cheek like a peach, like a peach,
  That is waiting for you in the church; —
But he clings to your side like a leech, like a leech,
  And you leave your lost bride in the lurch.

— There 's a babe in a fit, — hurry quick! hurry quick!
  To the doctor's as fast as you can!
The baby is off, while you stick, while you stick,
  In the grip of the dreadful Old Man!

— I have looked on the face of the Bore, of the Bore;
  The voice of the Simple I know;

I have welcomed the Flat at my door, at my door;
   I have sat by the side of the Slow;

I have walked like a lamb by the friend, by the friend,
   That stuck to my skirts like a bur;
I have borne the stale talk without end, without end,
   Of the sitter whom nothing could stir:

But my hamstrings grow loose, and I shake, and I shake,
   At the sight of the dreadful Old Man;
Yea, I quiver and quake, and I take, and I take,
   To my legs with what vigor I can!

O the dreadful Old Man of the Sea, of the Sea!
   He 's come back like the Wandering Jew!
He has had his cold claw upon me, upon me, —
   And be sure that he 'll have it on you!

ODE FOR A SOCIAL MEETING.

WITH SLIGHT ALTERATIONS BY A TEETOTALER.

COME! fill a fresh bumper, — for why should we go
   While the ~~nectar~~ logwood still reddens our cups as they flow;
Pour out the ~~rich juices~~ decoction still bright with the sun,
Till o'er the brimmed crystal the ~~rubies~~ dye-stuff shall run.

half-ripened apples
The ~~purple globed clusters~~ their life-dews have bled;
taste / sugar of lead
How sweet is the ~~breath~~ of the ~~fragrance they shed~~!
rank poisons / *wines!!!*
For summer's ~~last roses~~ lie hid in the ~~wines~~
stable-boys smoking long-nines
That were garnered by ~~maidens who laughed thro' the vines~~.

scowl / howl / scoff / sneer
Then a ~~smile~~, and a ~~glass~~, and a ~~toast~~, and a ~~cheer~~,
strychnine and whiskey, and ratsbane and beer
For all ~~the good wine, and we 've come of it here~~!
In cellar, in pantry, in attic, in hall,
Down, down with the tyrant that masters us all!
~~Long live the gay servant that laughs for us all~~!

PARSON TURELL'S LEGACY:

OR, THE PRESIDENT'S OLD ARM-CHAIR.

A MATHEMATICAL STORY.

FACTS respecting an old arm-chair.
At Cambridge. Is kept in the College there.
Seems but little the worse for wear.
That 's remarkable when I say
It was old in President Holyoke's day.
(One of his boys, perhaps you know,
Died, *at one hundred*, years ago.)
He took lodgings for rain or shine
Under green bed-clothes in '69.

Know old Cambridge? Hope you do. —
Born there? Don't say so! I was, too.
(Born in a house with a gambrel-roof, —
Standing still, if you must have proof. —
"Gambrel? — Gambrel?" — Let me beg
You 'll look at a horse's hinder leg, —
First great angle above the hoof, —
That 's the gambrel; hence gambrel-roof.)
— Nicest place that ever was seen, —
Colleges red and Common green,
Sidewalks brownish with trees between.
Sweetest spot beneath the skies
When the canker-worms don't rise, —
When the dust, that sometimes flies
Into your mouth and ears and eyes,
In a quiet slumber lies,
Not in the shape of unbaked pies
Such as barefoot children prize.

A kind of harbor it seems to be,
Facing the flow of a boundless sea.
Rows of gray old Tutors stand
Ranged like rocks above the sand;
Rolling beneath them, soft and green,
Breaks the tide of bright sixteen, —
One wave, two waves, three waves, four, —
Sliding up the sparkling floor:
Then it ebbs to flow no more,
Wandering off from shore to shore
With its freight of golden ore!
— Pleasant place for boys to play; —
Better keep your girls away;
Hearts get rolled as pebbles do
Which countless fingering waves pursue,

And every classic beach is strown
With heart-shaped pebbles of blood-red stone.

But this is neither here nor there; —
I 'm talking about an old arm-chair.
You 've heard, no doubt, of PARSON TURELL?
Over at Medford he used to dwell;
Married one of the Mathers' folk;
Got with his wife a chair of oak, —
Funny old chair with seat like wedge,
Sharp behind and broad front edge, —
One of the oddest of human things,
Turned all over with knobs and rings, —
But heavy, and wide, and deep, and grand, —
Fit for the worthies of the land, —
Chief Justice Sewall a cause to try in,
Or Cotton Mather to sit — and lie — in.
— Parson Turell bequeathed the same
To a certain student, — SMITH by name;
These were the terms, as we are told:
"Saide Smith saide Chaire to have and holde;
When he doth graduate, then to passe
To ye oldest Youth in ye Senior Classe.
On Payment of" — (naming a certain sum) —
"By him to whom ye Chaire shall come;
He to ye oldest Senior next,
And soe forever," — (thus runs the text,) —
"But one Crown lesse then he gave to claime,
That being his Debte for use of same."

Smith transferred it to one of the BROWNS,
And took his money, — five silver crowns.
Brown delivered it up to MOORE,
Who paid, it is plain, not five, but four.

Moore made over the chair to Lee,
Who gave him crowns of silver three.
Lee conveyed it unto Drew,
And now the payment, of course, was two.
Drew gave up the chair to Dunn, —
All he got, as you see, was one.
Dunn released the chair to Hall,
And got by the bargain no crown at all.
— And now it passed to a second Brown,
Who took it and likewise *claimed a crown.*
When *Brown* conveyed it unto Ware,
Having had one crown, to make it fair,
He paid him two crowns to take the chair;
And *Ware*, being honest, (as all Wares be,)
He paid one Potter, who took it, three.
Four got Robinson; five got Dix;
Johnson *primus* demanded six;
And so the sum kept gathering still
Till after the battle of Bunker's Hill.

— When paper money became so cheap,
Folks would n't count it, but said "a heap,"
A certain Richards, — the books declare, —
(A. M. in '90? I 've looked with care
Through the Triennial, — *name not there*,) —
This person, Richards, was offered then
Eight score pounds, but would have ten;
Nine, I think, was the sum he took, —
Not quite certain, — but see the book.
— By and by the wars were still,
But nothing had altered the Parson's will.
The old arm-chair was solid yet,
But saddled with such a monstrous debt!

Things grew quite too bad to bear,
Paying such sums to get rid of the chair!
But dead men's fingers hold awful tight,
And there was the will in black and white,
Plain enough for a child to spell.
What should be done no man could tell,
For the chair was a kind of nightmare curse,
And every season but made it worse.

As a last resort, to clear the doubt,
They got old GOVERNOR HANCOCK out.
The Governor came with his Light-horse Troop
And his mounted truckmen, all cock-a-hoop;
Halberds glittered and colors flew,
French horns whinnied and trumpets blew,
The yellow fifes whistled beneath their teeth
And the bumble-bee bass-drums boomed beneath;
So he rode with all his band,
Till the President met him, cap in hand.
— The Governor "hefted" the crowns, and said, —
"A will is a will, and the Parson 's dead."
The Governor hefted the crowns. Said he, —
"There is your p'int. And here 's my fee.
These are the terms you must fulfil, —
On such conditions I BREAK THE WILL!"
The Governor mentioned what these should be.
(Just wait a minute and then you 'll see.)
The President prayed. Then all was still,
And the Governor rose and BROKE THE WILL!
— "About those conditions?" Well, now you go
And do as I tell you, and then you 'll know.
Once a year, on Commencement day,
If you 'll only take the pains to stay,

You 'll see the President in the CHAIR,
Likewise the Governor sitting there.
The President rises; both old and young
May hear his speech in a foreign tongue,
The meaning whereof, as lawyers swear,
Is this: Can I keep this old arm-chair?
And then his Excellency bows,
As much as to say that he allows.
The Vice-Gub. next is called by name;
He bows like t' other, which means the same.
And all the officers round 'em bow,
As much as to say that *they* allow.
And a lot of parchments about the chair
Are handed to witnesses then and there,
And then the lawyers hold it clear
That the chair is safe for another year.

God bless you, Gentlemen! Learn to give
Money to colleges while you live.
Don't be silly and think you 'll try
To bother the colleges, when you die,
With codicil this, and codicil that,
That Knowledge may starve while Law grows fat;
For there never was pitcher that would n't spill,
And there 's always a flaw in a donkey's will!

CONTENTMENT.

"Man wants but little here below."

LITTLE I ask; my wants are few;
I only wish a hut of stone,
(A *very plain* brown stone will do,)
That I may call my own; —
And close at hand is such a one,
In yonder street that fronts the sun.

Plain food is quite enough for me;
Three courses are as good as ten; —
If Nature can subsist on three,
Thank Heaven for three. Amen!
I always thought cold victual nice; —
My *choice* would be vanilla-ice.

I care not much for gold or land; —
Give me a mortgage here and there, —
Some good bank-stock, — some note of hand,
Or trifling railroad share, —
I only ask that Fortune send
A *little* more than I shall spend.

Honors are silly toys, I know,
And titles are but empty names;
I would, *perhaps*, be Plenipo, —
But only near St. James;
I 'm very sure I should not care
To fill our Gubernator's chair.

Jewels are bawbles; 't is a sin
  To care for such unfruitful things; —
One good-sized diamond in a pin, —
    Some, *not so large*, in rings, —
A ruby, and a pearl, or so,
Will do for me; — I laugh at show.

My dame should dress in cheap attire;
  (Good, heavy silks are never dear;) —
I own perhaps I *might* desire
    Some shawls of true Cashmere, —
Some marrowy crapes of China silk,
Like wrinkled skins on scalded milk.

I would not have the horse I drive
  So fast that folks must stop and stare;
An easy gait — two, forty-five —
    Suits me; I do not care; —
Perhaps, for just a *single spurt*,
Some seconds less would do no hurt.

Of pictures, I should like to own
  Titians and Raphaels three or four, —
I love so much their style and tone, —
    One Turner, and no more,
(A landscape, — foreground golden dirt, —
The sunshine painted with a squirt.)

Of books but few, — some fifty score
  For daily use, and bound for wear;
The rest upon an upper floor; —
    Some *little* luxury *there*
Of red morocco's gilded gleam,
And vellum rich as country cream.

Busts, cameos, gems, — such things as these,
  Which others often show for pride,
I value for their power to please,
      And selfish churls deride; —
One Stradivarius, I confess,
Two Meerschaums, I would fain possess.

Wealth's wasteful tricks I will not learn,
  Nor ape the glittering upstart fool; —
Shall not carved tables serve my turn,
      But *all* must be of buhl?
Give grasping pomp its double share, —
I ask but *one* recumbent chair.

Thus humble let me live and die,
  Nor long for Midas' golden touch;
If Heaven more generous gifts deny,
      I shall not miss them *much*, —
Too grateful for the blessing lent
Of simple tastes and mind content!

DE SAUTY.

AN ELECTRO-CHEMICAL ECLOGUE.

Professor. *Blue-Nose.*

PROFESSOR.

TELL me, O Provincial! speak, Ceruleo-Nasal!
Lives there one De Sauty extant now among you,
Whispering Boanerges, son of silent thunder,
Holding talk with nations?

Is there a De Sauty ambulant on Tellus,
Bifid-cleft like mortals, dormient in night-cap,
Having sight, smell, hearing, food-receiving feature
Three times daily patent?

Breathes there such a being, O Ceruleo-Nasal?
Or is he a *mythus*, — ancient word for "humbug," —
Such as Livy told about the wolf that wet-nursed
Romulus and Remus?

Was he born of woman, this alleged De Sauty?
Or a living product of galvanic action,
Like the *acarus* bred in Crosse's flint-solution?
Speak, thou Cyano-Rhinal!

BLUE-NOSE.

Many things thou askest, jackknife-bearing stranger,
Much-conjecturing mortal, pork-and-treacle-waster!
Pretermit thy whittling, wheel thine ear-flap toward me,
Thou shalt hear them answered.

When the charge galvanic tingled through the cable,
At the polar focus of the wire electric
Suddenly appeared a white-faced man among us:
Called himself "DE SAUTY."

As the small opossum held in pouch maternal
Grasps the nutrient organ whence the term *mammalia*,
So the unknown stranger held the wire electric,
Sucking in the current.

When the current strengthened, bloomed the pale-faced stranger, —
Took no drink nor victual, yet grew fat and rosy, —
And from time to time, in sharp articulation,
Said, "*All right!* DE SAUTY."

From the lonely station passed the utterance, spreading
Through the pines and hemlocks to the groves of steeples,
Till the land was filled with loud reverberations
Of "*All right!* De Sauty."

When the current slackened, drooped the mystic stranger, —
Faded, faded, faded, as the stream grew weaker, —
Wasted to a shadow, with a hartshorn odor
Of disintegration.

Drops of deliquescence glistened on his forehead,
Whitened round his feet the dust of efflorescence,
Till one Monday morning, when the flow suspended,
There was no De Sauty.

Nothing but a cloud of elements organic,
C. O. H. N. Ferrum, Chlor. Flu. Sil. Potassa,
Calc. Sod. Phosph. Mag. Sulphur, Mang. (?) Alumin. (?) Cuprum, (?)
Such as man is made of.

Born of stream galvanic, with it he had perished!
There is no De Sauty now there is no current!
Give us a new cable, then again we 'll hear him
Cry, "*All right!* De Sauty."

ÆSTIVATION.

AN UNPUBLISHED POEM, BY MY LATE LATIN TUTOR.

IN candent ire the solar splendor flames;
The foles, languescent, pend from arid rames;
His humid front the cive, anheling, wipes,
And dreams of erring on ventiferous ripes.

How dulce to vive occult to mortal eyes,
Dorm on the herb with none to supervise,
Carp the suave berries from the crescent vine,
And bibe the flow from longicaudate kine!

To me, alas! no verdurous visions come,
Save yon exiguous pool's conferva-scum, —
No concave vast repeats the tender hue
That laves my milk-jug with celestial blue!

Me wretched! Let me curr to quercine shades!
Effund your albid hausts, lactiferous maids!
O, might I vole to some umbrageous clump, —
Depart, — be off, — excede, — evade, — erump!

THE OLD MAN DREAMS.

O FOR one hour of youthful joy!
Give back my twentieth spring!
I 'd rather laugh a bright-haired boy
Than reign a gray-beard king!

Off with the wrinkled spoils of age!
Away with learning's crown!
Tear out life's wisdom-written page,
And dash its trophies down!

One moment let my life-blood stream
From boyhood's fount of flame!
Give me one giddy, reeling dream
Of life all love and fame!

— My listening angel heard the prayer,
And, calmly smiling, said,
" If I but touch thy silvered hair,
Thy hasty wish hath sped.

" But is there nothing in thy track
To bid thee fondly stay,
While the swift seasons hurry back
To find the wished for day?"

— Ah, truest soul of womankind!
Without thee, what were life?
One bliss I cannot leave behind:
I 'll take — my — precious — wife!

— The angel took a sapphire pen
  And wrote in rainbow dew,
" The man would be a boy again,
  And be a husband too ! "

— " And is there nothing yet unsaid
  Before the change appears ?
Remember, all their gifts have fled
  With those dissolving years ! "

Why, yes ; for memory would recall
  My fond paternal joys ;
I could not bear to leave them all ;
  I 'll take — my — girl — and — boys !

The smiling angel dropped his pen, —
  " Why, this will never do ;
The man would be a boy again,
  And be a father too ! "

And so I laughed, — my laughter woke
  The household with its noise, —
And wrote my dream, when morning broke,
  To please the gray-haired boys.

WHAT WE ALL THINK.

THAT age was older once than now,
  In spite of locks untimely shed,
Or silvered on the youthful brow;
  That babes make love and children wed.

That sunshine had a heavenly glow,
  Which faded with those "good old days"
When winters came with deeper snow,
  And autumns with a softer haze.

That — mother, sister, wife, or child —
  The "best of women" each has known.
Were schoolboys ever half so wild?
  How young the grandpapas have grown!

That *but for this* our souls were free,
  And *but for that* our lives were blest;
That in some season yet to be
  Our cares will leave us time to rest.

Whene'er we groan with ache or pain, —
  Some common ailment of the race, —
Though doctors think the matter plain, —
  That ours is "a peculiar case."

That when like babes with fingers burned
  We count one bitter maxim more,
Our lesson all the world has learned,
  And men are wiser than before.

That when we sob o'er fancied woes,
  The angels hovering overhead
Count every pitying drop that flows,
  And love us for the tears we shed.

That when we stand with tearless eye
  And turn the beggar from our door,
They still approve us when we sigh,
  "Ah, had I but *one thousand more!*"

Though temples crowd the crumbled brink
  O'erhanging truth's eternal flow,
Their tablets bold with *what we think*,
  Their echoes dumb to *what we know;*

That one unquestioned text we read,
  All doubt beyond, all fear above,
Nor crackling pile nor cursing creed
  Can burn or blot it: GOD IS LOVE!

THE COMET.

THE Comet! He is on his way,
And singing as he flies;
The whizzing planets shrink before
The spectre of the skies;
Ah! well may regal orbs burn blue,
And satellites turn pale,
Ten million cubic miles of head,
Ten billion leagues of tail!

On, on by whistling spheres of light,
He flashes and he flames;
He turns not to the left nor right,
He asks them not their names;
One spurn from his demoniac heel,—
Away, away they fly,

Where darkness might be bottled up
And sold for "Tyrian dye."

And what would happen to the land,
And how would look the sea,
If in the bearded devil's path
Our earth should chance to be?
Full hot and high the sea would boil,
Full red the forests gleam;
Methought I saw and heard it all
In a dyspeptic dream!

I saw a tutor take his tube
The Comet's course to spy;
I heard a scream, — the gathered rays
Had stewed the tutor's eye;
I saw a fort, — the soldiers all
Were armed with goggles green;
Pop cracked the guns! whiz flew the balls!
Bang went the magazine!

I saw a poet dip a scroll
Each moment in a tub,
I read upon the warping back,
"The Dream of Beelzebub";
He could not see his verses burn,
Although his brain was fried,
And ever and anon he bent
To wet them as they dried.

I saw the scalding pitch roll down
The crackling, sweating pines,
And streams of smoke, like water-spouts,
Burst through the rumbling mines;

I asked the firemen why they made
Such noise about the town;
They answered not, — but all the while
The brakes went up and down.

I saw a roasting pullet sit
Upon a baking egg;
I saw a cripple scorch his hand
Extinguishing his leg;
I saw nine geese upon the wing
Towards the frozen pole,
And every mother's gosling fell
Crisped to a crackling coal.

I saw the ox that browsed the grass
Writhe in the blistering rays,
The herbage in his shrinking jaws
Was all a fiery blaze;
I saw huge fishes, boiled to rags,
Bob through the bubbling brine;
And thoughts of supper crossed my soul;
I had been rash at mine.

Strange sights! strange sounds! O fearful dream!
Its memory haunts me still,
The steaming sea, the crimson glare,
That wreathed each wooded hill;
Stranger! if through thy reeling brain
Such midnight visions sweep,
Spare, spare, O spare thine evening meal,
And sweet shall be thy sleep!

THE LAST BLOSSOM.

THOUGH young no more, we still would dream
  Of beauty's dear deluding wiles;
The leagues of life to graybeards seem
  Shorter than boyhood's lingering miles.

Who knows a woman's wild caprice?
  It played with Goethe's silvered hair,
And many a Holy Father's "niece"
  Has softly smoothed the papal chair.

When sixty bids us sigh in vain
  To melt the heart of sweet sixteen,
We think upon those ladies twain
  Who loved so well the tough old Dean.

We see the Patriarch's wintry face,
  The maid of Egypt's dusky glow,
And dream that Youth and Age embrace,
  As April violets fill with snow.

Tranced in her lord's Olympian smile
  His lotus-loving Memphian lies,—
The musky daughter of the Nile,
  With plaited hair and almond eyes.

Might we but share one wild caress
  Ere life's autumnal blossoms fall,
And Earth's brown, clinging lips impress
  The long cold kiss that waits us all!

My bosom heaves, remembering yet
  The morning of that blissful day,
When Rose, the flower of spring, I met,
  And gave my raptured soul away.

Flung from her eyes of purest blue,
  A lasso, with its leaping chain,
Light as a loop of larkspurs, flew
  O'er sense and spirit, heart and brain.

Thou com'st to cheer my waning age,
  Sweet vision, waited for so long!
Dove that would seek the poet's cage
  Lured by the magic breath of song!

She blushes! Ah, reluctant maid,
  Love's *drapeau rouge* the truth has told!
O'er girlhood's yielding barricade
  Floats the great Leveller's crimson fold!

Come to my arms! — love heeds not years;
  No frost the bud of passion knows. —
Ha! what is this my frenzy hears?
  A voice behind me uttered, — Rose!

Sweet was her smile, — but not for me;
  Alas! when woman looks *too* kind,
Just turn your foolish head and see, —
  Some youth is walking close behind!

"THE BOYS."

HAS there any old fellow got mixed with the boys?
If there has, take him out, without making a noise.
Hang the Almanac's cheat and the Catalogue's spite!
Old Time is a liar! We 're twenty to-night!

We 're twenty! We 're twenty! Who says we are more?
He 's tipsy, — young jackanapes! — show him the door!
"Gray temples at twenty?" — Yes! white if we please;
Where the snow-flakes fall thickest there 's nothing can freeze!

Was it snowing I spoke of? Excuse the mistake!
Look close, — you will see not a sign of a flake!
We want some new garlands for those we have shed, —
And these are white roses in place of the red.

We 've a trick, we young fellows, you may have been told,
Of talking (in public) as if we were old: —
That boy we call "Doctor," and this we call "Judge";
It 's a neat little fiction, — of course it 's all fudge.

That fellow 's the "Speaker," — the one on the right;
"Mr. Mayor," my young one, how are you to-night?
That 's our "Member of Congress," we say when we chaff;
There 's the "Reverend" What 's his name? — don't make me laugh.

That boy with the grave mathematical look
Made believe he had written a wonderful book,
And the ROYAL SOCIETY thought it was *true!*
So they chose him right in, — a good joke it was too!

There 's a boy, we pretend, with a three-decker brain,
That could harness a team with a logical chain;
When he spoke for our manhood in syllabled fire,
We called him " The Justice," but now he 's " The Squire."

And there 's a nice youngster of excellent pith, —
Fate tried to conceal him by naming him Smith;
But he shouted a song for the brave and the free, —
Just read on his medal, " My country," " of thee!"

You hear that boy laughing? — You think he 's all fun;
But the angels laugh, too, at the good he has done;
The children laugh loud as they troop to his call,
And the poor man that knows him laughs loudest of all!

Yes, we 're boys, — always playing with tongue or with pen;
And I sometimes have asked, Shall we ever be men?
Shall we always be youthful, and laughing, and gay,
Till the last dear companion drops smiling away?

Then here 's to our boyhood, its gold and its gray!
The stars of its winter, the dews of its May!
And when we have done with our life-lasting toys,
Dear Father, take care of thy children, THE BOYS!

January 6, 1859.

A SEA DIALOGUE.

Cabin Passenger. *Man at Wheel.*

CABIN PASSENGER.

FRIEND, you seem thoughtful. I not wonder much
That he who sails the ocean should be sad.
I am myself reflective. — When I think
Of all this wallowing beast, the Sea, has sucked
Between his sharp, thin lips, the wedgy waves,
What heaps of diamonds, rubies, emeralds, pearls;
What piles of shekels, talents, ducats, crowns,
What bales of Tyrian mantles, Indian shawls,
Of laces that have blanked the weavers' eyes,
Of silken tissues, wrought by worm and man,
The half-starved workman, and the well-fed worm;
What marbles, bronzes, pictures, parchments, books;
What many-lobuled, thought-engendering brains;
Lie with the gaping sea-shells in his maw, —
I, too, am silent; for all language seems
A mockery, and the speech of man is vain.
O mariner, we look upon the waves
And they rebuke our babbling. "Peace!" they say, —
"Mortal, be still!" My noisy tongue is hushed,
And with my trembling finger on my lips
My soul exclaims in ecstasy —

MAN AT WHEEL.

Belay

CABIN PASSENGER.

Ah yes! "Delay," — it calls, "nor haste to break
The charm of stillness with an idle word!"

O mariner, I love thee, for thy thought
Strides even with my own, nay, flies before.
Thou art a brother to the wind and wave;
Have they not music for thine ear as mine,
When the wild tempest makes thy ship his lyre,
Smiting a cavernous basso from the shrouds
And climbing up his gamut through the stays,
Through buntlines, bowlines, ratlines, till it shrills
An alto keener than the locust sings,
And all the great Æolian orchestra
Storms out its mad sonata in the gale
Is not the scene a wondrous and —

MAN AT WHEEL.

Avast!

CABIN PASSENGER.

Ah yes, a vast, a vast and wondrous scene!
I see thy soul is open as the day
That holds the sunshine in its azure bowl
To all the solemn glories of the deep.
Tell me, O mariner, dost thou never feel
The grandeur of thine office, — to control
The keel that cuts the ocean like a knife
And leaves a wake behind it like a seam
In the great shining garment of the world?

MAN AT WHEEL.

Belay y'r jaw, y' swab! y' hoss-marine!
(*To the Captain.*)
Ay, ay, Sir! Stiddy, Sir! Sou'wes' b' sou'!

November 10, 1864.

THE JUBILEE.

NAUTICUS LOQUITUR.

I 'VE heerd some talk of a Jubilee
To celebrate " our " " victory " ; —
Now I 'm a chap as follers the sea,
'n' f'r 'z I know, nob'dy 'll listen to me,
B't I 'll tell y' jest what 's my idee.

When you 'n' a fellah 'z got your grip,
Before y' 've settled it which can whip,
I won't say nothin'. You let her rip!
Knock him to pieces, chip by chip!
But don't fire into a sinkin' ship!

I tell y', shipmates 'n' lan'sm'n too,
There 's chaps aboard th't 's 'z good 'z you, —
'T was God A'mighty that made her crew!
FOLKS is FOLKS! 'n' that 's 'z true
'z that land is black 'n' water blue!

Come tell us, shipmates, ef y' can,
Was there ever a crew sence th' worl' began
That sech a wallopin' had to stan'
'z them poor fellahs th't tried t' man
The great Chicago catamaran!

Wahl, this is what y' 've hed t' do, —
T' lick 'em, — but not t' drown 'em too
There 's some good fellahs, 'n' not a few
That 's a swimmin' about, all chilled 'n' blue,
'n wants t' be h'isted aboard o' you!

Come, drowning foes! your friends we 'll be, —
We 've licked! Haw! haw! You 're licked! Hee! hee!
Hooraw for you! Hooraw for we!
We 'll wait till the whole wide land is free,
And then we 'll have our JUBILEE!

November 12, 1864.

THE SWEET LITTLE MAN.

DEDICATED TO THE STAY-AT-HOME RANGERS.

NOW, while our soldiers are fighting our battles,
  Each at his post to do all that he can,
Down among rebels and contraband chattels,
  What are you doing, my sweet little man?

All the brave boys under canvas are sleeping,
  All of them pressing to march with the van,
Far from the home where their sweethearts are weeping;
  What are you waiting for, sweet little man?

You with the terrible warlike moustaches,
  Fit for a colonel or chief of a clan,
You with the waist made for sword-belts and sashes,
  Where are your shoulder-straps, sweet little man?

Bring him the buttonless garment of woman!
  Cover his face lest it freckle and tan;
Muster the Apron-string Guards on the Common,
  That is the corps for the sweet little man!

Give him for escort a file of young misses,
Each of them armed with a deadly rattan;
They shall defend him from laughter and hisses,
Aimed by low boys at the sweet little man!

All the fair maidens about him shall cluster,
Pluck the white feathers from bonnet and fan,
Make him a plume like a turkey-wing duster, —
That is the crest for the sweet little man!

O, but the Apron-string Guards are the fellows!
Drilling each day since our troubles began, —
"Handle your walking-sticks!" "Shoulder umbrellas!"
That is the style for the sweet little man.

Have we a nation to save? In the first place
Saving ourselves is the sensible plan, —
Surely the spot where there 's shooting 's the worst place
Where I can stand, says the sweet little man.

Catch me confiding my person with strangers!
Think how the cowardly Bull-Runners ran!
In the brigade of the Stay-at-home Rangers
Marches my corps, says the sweet little man.

Such was the stuff of the Malakoff-takers,
Such were the soldiers that scaled the Redan;
Truculent housemaids and bloodthirsty Quakers,
Brave not the wrath of the sweet little man!

Yield him the sidewalk, ye nursery maidens!
Sauve qui peut! Bridget, and right about! Ann; —
Fierce as a shark in a school of menhadens,
See him advancing, the sweet little man!

When the red flails of the battle-field's threshers
Beat out the continent's wheat from its bran,
While the wind scatters the chaffy seceshers,
What will become of our sweet little man?

When the brown soldiers come back from the borders,
How will he look while his features they scan?
How will he feel when he gets marching orders,
Signed by his lady love? sweet little man!

Fear not for him, though the rebels expect him, —
  Life is too precious to shorten its span;
Woman her broomstick shall raise to protect him,
  Will she not fight for the sweet little man!

Now then, nine cheers for the Stay-at-home Ranger!
  Blow the great fish-horn and beat the big pan!
First in the field that is farthest from danger,
  Take your white-feather plume, sweet little man!

OUR OLDEST FRIEND.

READ TO "THE BOYS OF '29," JAN. 5, 1865.

I GIVE you the health of the oldest friend
That, short of eternity, earth can lend, —
A friend so faithful and tried and true
That nothing can wean him from me and you.

When first we screeched in the sudden blaze
Of the daylight's blinding and blasting rays,
And gulped at the gaseous, groggy air,
This old, old friend stood waiting there.

And when, with a kind of mortal strife,
We had gasped and choked into breathing life,
He watched by the cradle, day and night,
And held our hands till we stood upright.

From gristle and pulp our frames have grown
To stringy muscle and solid bone;
While we were changing, he altered not;
We might forget, but he never forgot.

He came with us to the college class, —
Little cared he for the steward's pass!
All the rest must pay their fee,
But the grim old dead-head entered free.

He stayed with us while we counted o'er
Four times each of the seasons four;
And with every season, from year to year,
The dear name Classmate he made more dear.

He never leaves us, — he never will,
Till our hands are cold and our hearts are still;
On birthdays, and Christmas, and New-Year's too,
He always remembers both me and you.

Every year this faithful friend
His little present is sure to send;
Every year, wheresoe'er we be,
He wants a keepsake from you and me.

How he loves us! he pats our heads,
And, lo! they are gleaming with silver threads;
And he 's always begging one lock of hair,
Till our shining crowns have nothing to wear.

At length he will tell us, one by one,
"My child, your labor on earth is done;
And now you must journey afar to see
My elder brother, — Eternity!"

And so, when long, long years have passed,
Some dear old fellow will be the last, —
Never a boy alive but he
Of all our goodly company!

When he lies down, but not till then,
Our kind Class-Angel will drop the pen
That writes in the day-book kept above
Our lifelong record of faith and love.

So here 's a health in homely rhyme
To our oldest classmate, Father Time!
May our last survivor live to be
As bald, but as wise and tough as he!

A FAREWELL TO AGASSIZ.

HOW the mountains talked together,
Looking down upon the weather,
When they heard our friend had planned his
Little trip among the Andes!
How they 'll bare their snowy scalps
To the climber of the Alps
When the cry goes through their passes,
"Here comes the great Agassiz!"
"Yes, I 'm tall," says Chimborazo,
"But I wait for him to say so, —
That 's the only thing that lacks, — he
Must see me, Cotopaxi!"

"Ay! ay!" the fire-peak thunders,
"And he must view my wonders!
I 'm but a lonely crater
Till I have him for spectator!"
The mountain hearts are yearning,
The lava-torches burning,
The rivers bend to meet him,
The forests bow to greet him,
It thrills the spinal column
Of fossil fishes solemn,
And glaciers crawl the faster
To the feet of their old master!

Heaven keep him well and hearty,
Both him and all his party!
From the sun that broils and smites,
From the centipede that bites,
From the hail-storm and the thunder,
From the vampire and the condor,
From the gust upon the river,
From the sudden earthquake shiver,
From the trip of mule or donkey,
From the midnight howling monkey,
From the stroke of knife or dagger,
From the puma, and the jaguar,
From the horrid boa-constrictor
That has scared us in the pictur',
From the Indians of the Pampas
Who would dine upon their grampas,
From every beast and vermin
That to think of sets us squirming,
From every snake that tries on
The traveller his p'ison,

From every pest of Natur',
Likewise the alligator,
And from two things left behind him, —
(Be sure they 'll try to find him,)
The tax-bill and assessor, —
Heaven keep the great Professor!

May he find, with his apostles,
That the land is full of fossils,
That the waters swarm with fishes
Shaped according to his wishes,
That every pool is fertile
In fancy kinds of turtle,
New birds around him singing,
New insects, never stinging,
With a million novel data
About the articulata,
And facts that strip off all husks
From the history of mollusks.

And when, with loud Te Deum,
He returns to his Museum,
May he find the monstrous reptile
That so long the land has kept ill
By Grant and Sherman throttled,
And by Father Abraham bottled,
(All specked and streaked and mottled
With the scars of murderous battles,
Where he clashed the iron rattles
That gods and men he shook at,)
For all the world to look at!

God bless the great Professor!
And Madam too, God bless her!

Bless him and all his band,
On the sea and on the land,
As they sail, ride, walk, and stand, —
Bless them head and heart and hand,
Till their glorious raid is o'er,
And they touch our ransomed shore!
Then the welcome of a nation,
With its shout of exultation,
Shall awake the dumb creation,
And the shapes of buried æons
Join the living creatures' pæans,
While the mighty megalosaurus
Leads the palæozoic chorus, —
God bless the great Professor,
And the land his proud possessor, —
Bless them now and evermore!

Cambridge: Printed by Welch, Bigelow, & Co.

www.ingramcontent.com/pod-product-compliance
Lightning Source LLC
LaVergne TN
LVHW020242110826
845151LV00003B/1004